e-Dapt

To our parents John & Nancy Corey- the inspiration for all we accomplish

Foreword

Can we talk? In this book you will learn the tricks of the trade and how new-wave marketers are making your Competitors Companies' achieve an advantage with your customers. The secret –the real secret –is that it is not done with smoke and mirrors but with old fashion hard work. This is what makes the difference between the fly-by-night SEO chasers and true digital marketers. Chris and Brian will explain the intricacies of how to effectively use modern tools to achieve market position change and why industry leaders are investing heavily in these forms of promotion.

The "Golden Rule" of Sales and Marketing will always be that customers buy from people they like and people who make their lives easier or help them do their job. Whether that is done by personal relationship building or by the ease of e-commerce, the sales results come from making sure your customers like your Company, that your products add value to their lives, and that it is easy and enjoyable for them to get what they desire.

The challenge is to find the confluence between modern digital wizardry and the basic principles of marketing that have worked for so long. "Rosie the Riveter" convinced six million women to join the workforce in World War II with zero dollars spent on pay-per-click. Today political candidates would not think of running a Campaign without social media as a major component.

As a 58-year-old Sales and Marketing Executive who is struggling through the digital revolution, and daily trying to transition to this new blinking lights world, who do I trust to bring modern tools – like social media, e-commerce, search engines, and pay-per-click— to properly tell the story and represent my company's business interests? How do I apply the tried-and-true principles of Sales and Marketing to this new media? Do I completely move my Print, TV, and Direct mail marketing budgets into digital marketing, or is there a balance that maximizes the benefit?

My business goal, as always, is to identify my markets, target particular sectors, find the potential customer base, and get them to raise their hands so the selling can begin. Google, Bing, and Yahoo are the Yellow Pages and Thomas' Register of the new marketing world, and customers search there moments after the thought has crossed their minds. The Internet has to be where my efforts and marketing investment are focused. If I want to be number one in my market, I have to be number one on these search engines.

Digital Marketers are the "Mad Men" of this generation and in this book, Brian and Chris will explain how this work is done correctly and with efficacy. I think you will be surprised that the tricks of the trade come with mountains of effort to achieve results. Enjoy "e-dapt".

John Corey

I. ADAPT
- Luddites and the Rise of Digital Marketing
- Luddites and the Radio
- The Three Screens

II. SHIFTS IN MARKETING
- The Beginning
- The Softer Side
- The Power of Visuals
- Take Control
- Return on Investment
- The Final Frontier

III. REALIZING THE EXISTENCE OF THE WEB
- Compete or Leave Business on the Table
- SEO, PPC, and Other Distracting Buzzwords
- What Do You Need?
- Goals and Completing Them
- Word of Mouth Marketing

IV. PRACTICAL BUDGETING – THE INTERNET IS NOT EASY MONEY
- Not Easy Money - Earned Money
- Growth: Advertising vs. Organic
- The Myth of "Launch and Thrive"
- Traffic Isn't Always the #1 Goal
- The Importance of Branding

V. WEB SITES

- Getting a Useful Website
- Click Through and Lead Generation
- How Much to Pay for a Website
- Where Do Visitors Come From?
- Modern Sharing Model
- Olive Branches and Arms – When to Collaborate and When to Destroy
- A/B Testing
- Set Goals

VI. SOCIAL MEDIA

- Cultivating your Brand[ed Traffic]
- Don't Spend Too Much Time on Social Media
- Growth: Organic, Churning, and Purchasing
- Links from Social Media
- Honesty
- It's About People

VII. SEARCH ENGINES

- How to Get in Their Good Graces
- Their Business Is Your Business
- The Two Faces of Googleplex
- Don't Forget Bing and Yahoo Just Because Everyone Else Has
- Pay Per Click

VIII. GOING DEEPER INTO THE DATA

- Automation Saves Time and Your Business

IX. CLOSING

I. Adapt

When the right catalyst comes along, the world has a tendency to change forever. In the late nineteenth century, the invention of the engine was one such catalyst. During the six-month period that the engine was on display at the 1876 World's Fair, ten million people visited the exposition – at a time when travel was extremely difficult – and had their lives completely changed. Technology was no longer a flight of fancy; it was a life-improving reality. The engine hailed the age of steam technology, telegraphs, railroads, and mass production. Society evolved rapidly, both culturally and economically, businesses adapted, and people surrendered to the tide of technology or became footnotes in history. As was the case in the Industrial Revolution, in this new Digital Revolution business owners must harness the power of the *search* engine or resign their businesses to ignominious fates.

The sheer disruptive quality of the Industrial Revolution was daunting to some, but they absolutely had to get with the times. In today's ongoing Digital Revolution, history is repeating itself. It is axiomatic that the Digital Revolution has disrupted the status quo. Baby Boomers, whose first cellular phones were the size of a brick, are now walking around with palm-sized smart phones with more computing power than all of NASA during the Apollo 11 mission. Every one of us is constantly connected to the world via our phone. We all know at least a few people who don't even roll out of bed before checking their phones. The thought of losing our smart phones brings about an acute sense of panic because they have become an integral part of our everyday lives. Devices may change, but their intent never does. Machinery from 1876 to now should make our lives easier and more connected. Marketing has never been more convenient or easier for those willing to adapt to the power of the search engine.

Luddites[1] and the Rise of Digital Marketing

A certain amount of push-back is inevitable when a truly disruptive technology comes along. A classic example is the Luddite movement of the early nineteenth century. The Luddites felt threatened by the wave of new machines the Industrial Revolution ushered into existence, and their knee-jerk reaction was to smash them to bits. While this was undoubtedly extreme, it is a distinctly human reaction that was designed to protect the only way of life - and means of supporting themselves - the Luddites knew. However, the most important takeaway from the Luddite movement is that it was ultimately futile. From the moment a new technology displaces an outdated method, there is simply no way of turning back the clock and reverting to a simpler time. Successful business owners must be cognizant of new technologies and incorporate them into their long-term vision for the

---

[1] The term "Luddite" refers to members of a group of activist textile artisans from the early nineteenth century who smashed newly-invented power looms and stocking frames, which, at the time, represented a dramatic upheaval of the textile industry that permitted business owners to replace skilled artisans with low-paid, unskilled, machine-tending laborers. In popular usage, the term is commonly used to refer to those who eschew new technologies in favor of tried-and-true methods, even if those methods are far less efficient.

future of their company at the earliest practicable date. Revolutionary technologies destroy the old way of life and instill a new order that is distinctly different - for better or worse.

Had they more foresight, the Luddites' reaction to the invention of the powered loom might have been far different. We are fortunate to live in an age when access to information is ubiquitous and the mistakes of our forebears have highlighted many a blind alley, which we can now avoid. With hindsight, we know that the average Luddite would have been far better off if his reaction had been to adapt to the new textile manufacturing environment by learning to build or operate power looms rather than to smash them. Informational hurdles commonly cause people to react in emotional ways – like the Luddites who didn't know what else to do – and, in this digital age, nothing is quite so costly as approaching your business matters in a similarly emotional way. It is crucial to be informed about what the internet can do for you so that you don't dismiss it out of hand based on an emotional reaction and a futile desire for simpler times.

New technologies are constantly creating brand new jobs while simultaneously rendering other jobs obsolete. There's just no getting around it. A decade ago, people could not fathom the idea of having a "social media specialist" on the payroll. Even suggesting it would have been met by strange looks and condescending laughs. The old standard marketing approach dominated, namely print, radio, and television marketing (i.e., low-tech and low-yield). Fast-forward to today and expertise in social media marketing is a qualification for many jobs.

Luddites and the Radio

As we discussed, disruptive technologies almost always instigate a certain amount of push-back from us because we feel comfortable with what we know at any given time. Everyone likes what is safe for him or her. Technology is an untamable force, and, based on our mistakes from the past, we know that our vision of the future is almost always imperfect. What we have to avoid, however, is allowing our knowledge of our imperfect foresight to translate into an inertia that keeps us stagnant. While there is nothing wrong with a healthy amount of skepticism for burgeoning technologies (anyone remember LaserDisc?), technologies that increase the connectedness of people are a horse of a different color, and it is vital that we make our decisions based on the information available to us and not our emotions.

There will always be Luddites. Every age has its naysayers. Before the first radio broadcasts were underwritten by advertisers in the early 1920s it was unthinkable that radio advertising would seriously displace print advertising. But, as the century rolled onward and radio became the dominant form of mass communication, with families sitting together in their living rooms to listen to their favorite programs all across the nation, marketing dollars flowed into radio advertising like a tidal wave. In comparison to modern advertising through television and the internet, we know that radio has its shortcomings, but it was easily the best option available to advertisers at the time. Indeed, as we learned later, there is nothing quite like the visceral reaction people have upon seeing a sleek new product on television for the first time, and this was something with which radio and print could just not compete.

The Three Screens

Perhaps the best way to think of the post-radio history of technology is through a Three Screen Revolution: television screen, computer screen, and smartphone screen. While this period was radically different from the ascendant period of the radio, the parallels are immediately apparent.

Like radio, television faced its own resistance when it raced onto the scene in the 1950s. The naysayers declared that radio was far too ingrained in the family life for any other medium to take over. People had their radio and the silver screen, after all - what else could they possibly need? Radio pioneers and personalities declared that television was a fad. There was just no way anyone could stare at a tiny screen on a talking pine box for longer than an hour at a time, they said.

As a radical new technology, television was in many cases initially dismissed or rejected in favor of radios, with which people had comfortable histories and fond memories. And it certainly didn't help that, like any new technology, television came with a few kinks, such as the need for television actors to wear green facial makeup and black lipstick to appear normal on black-and-white displays. However, as television grew more and more prominent as a medium, going from a few stations to the fastest growing new invention of its time, it became a force to be reckoned with for marketers.

Then came televised national events, which allowed people from small communities across the country to feel they were "right there" in the action, and television trumped radio forever. Television opened the world up for these small communities by showing them the world outside their sheltered homes. Life changed, especially among the young. Kids raced home after school to watch programs, and Saturday morning cartoons became an integral part of childhood. When grandparents tried to entice their grandkids into listening to the radio, they were met with protests of "that's boring."

If we think of the **market share**[2] each medium has for people's attention (limiting ourselves for the moment to television, radio, and print), it goes without saying that television has long since taken the top spot from radio and print, but neither radio nor print disappeared. In fact, in

---

[2] The term market share is typically used to refer to the slice of the total sales of any given industry or market (or in this case, people's attention) which a certain company controls. For instance, something like ninety-two percent of all computers use a Microsoft Windows operating system, five percent use Apple's OSX, and two percent use others. Microsoft's market share of the operating system market is ninety-two percent, Apple's is five percent, and so on.

conjunction, they can all help businesses. No medium which commands even a relatively small share of people's attention should be ignored. Radio and print advertising were still valuable in the age of the television – just as they are all valuable today.

To this mix we must, of course, add the computer. Before the advent of the internet, computers were initially unavailable as a marketing medium - unlike radio and television, which were connected to broadcast sources at inception. However, thanks to Al Gore's tireless efforts[3] the internet grew from a military-backed research project into an incredible new method for us civilians to share information with each other. As internet usage exploded across the world in the 1990s the world became a smaller place, globalization took on an entirely new meaning, and people became far more connected than ever before.

Television allowed everyone to have a unified visual, but the internet in many ways celebrates the individual while simultaneously reassuring individuals that they are not alone. Those with eclectic interests and hobbies were suddenly able to connect and form communities with others who have the same likes. Global niches began forming. Marketers, unaccustomed to this new medium, approached the internet clumsily. Pop-up advertisements often bombarded users every few seconds in ill-advised attempts to be like television commercials. Just like the period when marketers had to transition

---

[3] Please note: our tongues are firmly planted in our cheeks.

from radio to television, the gaffes proved to be powerful learning lessons, and ads were eventually toned down in favor of quality over quantity. The focus shifted to content rather than flash.

Cell phones improved alongside computers and internet accessibility. The huge bricks of the '80s vanished, and much sleeker (by comparison) second-generation cell phones with text capability appeared. Just a few years after that, cell phones stopped being over-priced status symbols and started being necessities for the modern person. By 2006 Research In Motion's revolutionary Blackberry devices enabled people to talk, text, and check their email on a single device. Our lives went from *wanting* a cell phone and a faster dial-up connection to *needing* a cell phone and a high-speed DSL connection. By 2007 the parallel evolutionary lines of computers, the internet, and cell phones merged and the smart phone was born. The same teenagers that flocked to the internet embraced the new systems of communication as adults. It was a near seamless transition for those already familiar with technology, but a majority of marketers have continued to hesitate to invest.

History repeats itself for those who are not willing to evolve, but those who are early to adapt to new mediums of communication reap the rewards and push humankind forward and closer together. Anything new meets with resistance throughout the ages, but the early adapters always flourish. Now, with just a little bit more knowledge, you can join in as well. If you feel that it's too late – you're wrong. There is still plenty of opportunity for late-comers on the internet. Consider the existing misallocation of marketing dollars: businesses *still* devote twenty-five times more marketing money to print advertising than to advertising through mobile devices (i.e., smart phones and tablets), yet modern humans spend more time engrossed in their mobile devices than reading print. At this point in the evolution of technology and communication, this is simply asinine. There is no good argument for not investing in internet marketing and the old "this is just how I've always done it" mentality is nothing but a detriment to your business. The cost of doing business should not make you the dunce or the Miss Havisham of radio.

The argument can be made: If internet marketing is such a force, then why doesn't everything related to social media and the internet take off? The answer is simple: not everything works and not everyone has the talent and vision to see things through to their potential. MySpace (a predecessor to Facebook) may not have had the wild success of Facebook, but it conclusively showed that people were interested in online social networking services. Facebook picked up where MySpace left off, monetized online social networking, and came to market in an initial public offering which peaked at a $104 billion market cap. Certain ideas may not work out, but the force of change is still in motion. The revolution will not only be televised (or, more likely, streamed on the internet), but viewers will have the capacity to have a dialogue about it in in a virtual environment in real-time with people from all over the world. The market is there - all you have to do is take a calculated risk to make it work for you. We promise your competitors are already doing so.

II. Shifts in Marketing

As long as people have had something to sell, there have been marketers. The original tactic was **outbound marketing**.[4] Traditionally, the company starts the conversation and does so through tradeshows, TV commercials, radio commercials and print advertisements such as newspaper ads, magazine ads, flyers, brochures, catalogs, cold calls, and e-mail blasts. This has always been largely ineffective, but it was the only way to do things until the vast potential of the internet was realized.

Business owners with a limited understanding of the comparative performance of differing marketing techniques often blindly allocate money to outbound marketing and chalk it up to one of the usual costs of business. However, we know that this is just another knee-jerk reaction to an informational hurdle. The challenges of outbound marketing are numerous, the results it generates are lackluster, and any rational business owner, with this information in hand, should eschew outbound marketing techniques in favor higher-yielding alternatives. For example, it is very difficult to track your ROI[5] on outbound marketing expenditures, the federal Do Not Call List

---

[4] With outbound marketing, advertisers try to find potential customers through print, radio, or television advertising, telemarketing, direct mailings of promotional materials, or by sending e-mails to large mailing lists (a.k.a. spam e-mail).
[5] ROI is short for "Return on Investment," an investment performance measure which is calculated by taking the total gain from an investment, subtracting the cost of that investment, and dividing the result by the cost of the investment. For example, if my internet marketing campaign generated $10 in sales, and cost my company $8 in total, then my internet marketing

hinders reaching potential customers on the phone, Digital Video Recorders ("DVR") connected to televisions (think: TiVo) allow commercials to be completely skipped over, e-mail accounts have near-impenetrable spam filters, and direct mailings rarely make it past the nearest trash can (unless the tray in the hamster's cage needs new lining). The result of these impediments to outbound marketing penetration is that the traditional methods have a high cost and a low yield.

Inbound marketing[6] is the polar opposite. With outbound marketing, advertisers are screaming for attention in an increasingly noisy world; the usual result of which is either driving potential customers away or being lost in the cacophony. With inbound marketing, advertisers set the stage in their favor so that potential customers seek them out through the crowd. You probably don't need us to tell you this, but people use Google (or Bing, if it was set as your default homepage and you don't know how to change it)[7] to find almost everything they need in their lives. Whether they are looking for the nearest tag agency to update their license plate, the nearest home goods store to pick up some kitchen knives, or the best breeder of rare pigs in West Virginia, chances are people are using a search engine to find it. The

---

campaign generated a healthy twenty percent return on my investment in internet marketing [($10 - $8) / $10 = .2].

[6] With inbound marketing, advertisers create content specifically designed to appeal to their potential customers, actively seek to make that content widely available to potential customers through various online sources, and then allow the content to draw the potential customers in to the advertiser's website.

[7] We can help you with that, too.

search engine has become synonymous with doing research. A potential buyer types in the keywords for what they are looking for and voila, pages of matching information appear. This is precisely the type of activity that inbound marketing seeks to capitalize upon.

The interaction with a potential customer in the typical inbound marketing scenario is as such: the customer starts the conversation by typing a few keywords into Google; Google happily provides advertisements and a list of websites related to those keywords to keep the conversation going; the customer clicks on an advertisement or a website that seems to suit their needs; and, finally, the customer arrives at a businesses' website as a **warm lead**.[8] The key difference in this scenario, as contrasted with outbound marketing efforts, is that the customer was fully in control of how they arrived as a potential customer. Rather than yielding under the combined weight of direct mailings and unsolicited phone calls (which, let's face it, is so very unlikely), the customer *chose* to come to the businesses' site. Now all the business must do is reciprocate the customer's interest by supplying a website that answers all of their questions satisfactorily (or, better yet, superbly), and they've got a sale in the bag. The most obvious takeaway from this scenario is: If you do not have a strong presence on the

---

[8] Warm leads are potential customers who come to you with an interest in having a conversation about your product or company, as contrasted with a cold lead, who has never heard of your product or company before and is usually far more difficult to convert into a sale (think about all the telemarketers you've slammed the phone on – you were a cold lead).

internet your competitors will be the ones capturing potential customers' attention simply by being the only one to have shown up on game day.

This is not to say that all you have to do is create a website and enjoy the free ride; as discussed later in this book: nothing comes for free. You've only managed to get your foot in the door for a sale by getting a potential customer to your website. It may be a warm lead that has landed on your digital doorstep, but they are anything but a sure thing, which is why internet marketing is so much more than just having a website that gets traffic. It goes without saying that you must have a presence on the internet to be in the game, but how well you do in the game is an entirely different story. We can help you, but your impact - your attractiveness to potential customers - is up to you. The first step is pushing the idea that your business "doesn't need the internet" out of your head, the second step is admitting you need help. Internet marketing can be a cash cow, but you need the right milk maid to get her to work for you.[9]

The Beginning

When the internet first came out, it was an extremely basic channel of communication. E-mails, conspiracy theories, chain letters, and increasingly odd chat rooms were just about the full extent of the internet's use until a new breed of marketing pioneer realized the vast potential and took action.

---

[9] Corey Consulting has been at it since 2011 with a ninety-four percent client retention rate, so we must be doing something right.

In 1994, the amount of money spent on internet marketing was practically zilch, but only one year later that number was $300 million.

Banner ads were among the first methods of web solicitation. As the name implies, these are simple, colorful links across the top or side of any given website that deliver a warm lead to a second website that paid to have their product or company advertised on the first website. As soon as banner ads started generating sales, interest in internet marketing took off. The realization that website traffic could be converted into cash through sales of advertising space was the impetus for the creation of search engines. There is nothing free about owning and running a search engine; there are costs associated with it at every step of the way. However, the pioneers who developed the first search engines realized that a simple way to generate extensive traffic was to provide a valuable (and free) service to get users to visit their website as often as possible. The traffic is then monetized, and all the associated costs of running the search engine paid (and a nice profit pulled in), by renting ad space (for banner ads, initially) and selling priority in search returns to advertisers.

Please note that search engines' ability to monetize web traffic does not negate our rule that "successful internet marketing is about far more than generating web traffic," because a search engine's business model is completely different than that of a business which is seeking to sell a product or service. And, the reality is that the rule is just reversed for search engines, not inapplicable. Think about it: a search engine's cash flow is dependent on traffic, and everybody has a favorite search engine to which they default, thus, to maximize traffic, search engines must be more appealing to users in some way that matters to people (be it through aesthetics, simplicity, or even appealing to peoples' green streak – the search engine www.ecosia.com donates eighty percent of its ad income to a tree planting program in Brazil).

Flash Software,[10] which made advertisements come alive, was the next big move in banner ads. Following on the heels of Flash were the so-called "interrupting ads" (i.e., those many, many, many, annoying pop-up ads you've closed in your lifetime), which are still used today, although most web browsers now contain prophylactic software designed to nip pop-ups in the bud to keep you sane. Interrupting ads are the internet's version of outbound marketing (along with spam e-mail, of course), and, unsurprisingly, are among the lowest-yielding methods of internet marketing.

The Softer Side

By the year 2000, a softer approach to internet marketing had taken hold. Marketers began inviting people to see advertisements rather than throwing them in their faces. Lucrative home-based startups, based on

---

[10] Flash Software is what was used to make banner ads come alive with rudimentary animations or videos; its usage on websites has been in decline for many years.

successful internet marketing, began popping up all over the place. While those with more money could advertise on a larger scale than small startups, everyone's products or services had the potential to be viewed. Anyone could sell anything legal over the web to fill some demand. Once again, the market was flooded and it was time to stand out in a crowded market. Then a curious thing happened, as they are wont to do.

Smart phones, the dark horse of internet marketing, upped the game for all involved. By 2010, ninety percent of households had a phone, but by 2011, one out of every two people had a smart phone. While the early days of smart phones initially posed a challenge for information gathering (filling out forms on early versions of smart phones was a nightmare we're sure you recall), auto-fill software that remembers personal information and supplies it instantly whenever an order form needs to be filled out has largely alleviated this headache. At the same time as the rise of smart phones, the age of social media took off, with young people spending significantly more time browsing the internet than watching television. MySpace, LinkedIn, and Facebook are all available on-the-go via smart phones. Everyone is plugged in, but they have become jaded with so many options and demands on their time and interests. While everyone's attention is accessible in the cyber world, they also do not want to be bombarded.

The once-bulky and simple devices of yore are now miniature computers that fit into a pocket. Internet marketing has progressed to the point that advertisements are less intrusive and often are just a small non-monetary cost associated with using what is an otherwise free application on your phone. You know what we're talking about: think of the free stock tracker you downloaded on your phone that displays small banner ads occasionally (or encourages you to upgrade to the Pro version for $3.99), the short advertisements that run every now and again while you listen to music on Pandora or Spotify, your GPS navigator that recommends nearby businesses for your patronage, or the . These advertisements probably don't even make you flinch (and certainly don't instill the eye-twitching madness of interrupting ads).

By 2012, social media and blogs[11] were generating leads and customers. As a result, marketers invested almost sixty percent more in social media marketing. The biggest challenge now is the attention span of the potential client. With so many three-ring circuses happening across the web, even a thirty-second pitch is too long and a forever-shortening attention span has become the enemy of a sale.

The Power of Visuals

Psychologist Albert Mehrabian demonstrated that ninety-three percent of communication is nonverbal, thus actions do scientifically speak louder

---

[11] "Blog" is short for web-log. A blog is just a website that is updated often through periodic postings, with older posts archived and available for a visitor to browse through. A business blog might have daily or weekly entries (posts), which summarize the big business news of the previous day or week; fashion blogs might post daily outfits; etc.

than words. This is not really surprising; the majority of human history occurred before we developed the ability to communicate with words or record our history with text. Even as infants we see before we can speak and the comparatively persuasive power of visuals over text does not really change throughout our lives. It is hardwired into our brains. It is proven that people retain data conveyed to them through visual communication better than data conveyed through text alone. **Native advertising**, which refers to advertising within a context, seeks to take advantage of this evolutionary predisposition (think of a starlet in a movie jumping into a sleek Audi or Mercedes and driving off). The websites Instagram and Pinterest, on which users each have their own mini-blogs upon which they post photographs, are prime examples of native advertising on the web. A person can say they love reading and long walks on the beach, but they can capture their essence in a single image. Think of the saturation of selfies[12] to advertise oneself in our increasingly visual world. Advertisers can do the same on these mediums.

There is a substantial market for every business on the web. Whether or not a business captures a piece of the pie is based on the owner's willingness to accept that the internet is where all new business development is going. The most incomprehensible thing we hear from business owners at Corey Consulting is that their business cannot benefit

---

[12] Per Wikipedia: A selfie is a self-portrait photograph, typically taken with a hand-held digital camera or camera phone, [which is] often shared on social networking services.

from the web. The instantaneous accessibility of smart phones immediately changed the landscape for marketing businesses. Smart phones are the yellow pages (to a higher order of magnitude), tucked neatly away in our pockets, they are alarm clocks, watches, a desktop computer, a calendar, a bank, a social network, and more. Smart phones have placed the world at consumers' fingertips, and now they want it all and they want it fast.

The new Digital Information Age makes adaptation a must. Most small businesses are either ignoring the call to change or not adapting at all for no good reason besides a sense of unease with rapidly changing technology. Outbound marketing is proven to be far less effective than inbound marketing. Don't let your business be left behind in this era of information. The idea that there are businesses that potentially cannot benefit from the internet is categorically incorrect. Not existing on the web is similar to not existing in the physical world. A quick, decisive way of determining the value of the web is to jump on a search engine, type in a few keywords related to your industry, and see your competitors actively soliciting business.

Take Control

There are numerous reasons to invest in internet marketing, but some of the most compelling are basic. While less true of Baby Boomers, much of Generation X has adapted comfortably to a lifestyle that includes the internet at every turn (even if sometimes clumsily so), the Millenials grew up in the age of the internet and use it for everything, and, lastly, the generation that is currently coming of age is damn near part cyborg (the proficiency with which we've seen toddlers manipulate tablets and smart phones shocks us). Every passing day and year, the demographics of the world are constantly shifting towards people being more and more digitally inclined. From an adapting older population to in-coming generations, some of your potential business is simply fixed to the web. You need to exist on the web to accommodate these individuals. Maybe your business falls under the category of having no proprietary web presence at all, but that doesn't mean it doesn't have a presence. In fact, if you are not actively curating your business presence on the web, someone else has likely beaten you to the punch. Review sites, social media, and even your direct competition create a presence for you on the web, whether you like it or not. Developing **proprietary resources**[13] is key to controlling your message on the web - unless you prefer having your competitors do it for you.

If you already have a proprietary web presence, it would be beneficial to expand. Fortunately, the internet lends itself to creativity and expanding your presence can be as simple as posting on Facebook consistently. Unlike the 'Mad Men' days of yore, social media updates that promote your

---

[13] Proprietary resources are websites, social media presences (think: Twitter, Instagram, Pinterest, and Facebook), and map listings that *you* control.

business need not be the product of weeks-long strategy development sessions and huge marketing budgets aimed at developing catchy jingles or phraseology, such as 'Got Milk?'[14]

Digital marketing can increase the bottom line. At Corey Consulting, we often hear new clients talk about "that time" when they sent out 5,000 postcards and got *one* new customer. Shockingly, they are thrilled at this **conversion rate!**[15] We would be absolutely ashamed if our conversion rates remotely approached such a low number. The exposure that we can generate for your business through a single blog is not only many orders of magnitude larger than what any direct mailing is capable of, but the shift from cold leads to warm leads yields massive increases in conversion rates. Adapt to the new ways of marketing to massively increase your ROI.

Why invest in internet marketing instead of other forms of marketing? It would be disingenuous to suggest that a business owner should not invest in other types of marketing. There is certainly a long history of proven (though low) ROI in television, radio, and print, and any business with the opportunity should move into those fields as well. However, a business can

---

[14] This is **not** meant to imply that your online presence should not be well thought out; companies get themselves in deep when they use social media recklessly. This will be discussed more later (with examples).

[15] Conversion rates are one of the most important metrics to determine the success of a marketing strategy. Calculating conversion rates is dependent on the goal of your campaign. In the example above, where a business owner was seeking to generate new customers by mailing postcards about his business to five thousand people, while only attracting one new customer, his conversion rate was 1/5000, or .0002 (that's two one-hundredths of one percent).

survive the changing times without investing in print, radio, and television, but the same is not true of internet marketing. Modern day businesses can't afford to skip over the internet as a marketing tool; to do so is to accept an ever-increasingly small market share - a death knell for any business.

The internet is a marketplace that is growing by the day (remember, people are becoming *more*, not less, digitally inclined), and it follows that the internet's impact on businesses is growing accordingly. While individuals propel this growth by allocating a greater and greater amount of their attention to online sources of information, concomitant voids are appearing in the traditional communications mediums like radio, television, and print: print newspapers are going out of business; and the web is absorbing radio, television, and even home phone service! The mediums through which businesses can communicate with their desired audience are depleting in favor of the internet. The sooner you get on board, the better.

It is crucial to understand your ROI, but it is difficult to get your hands on the information to calculate it through the traditional marketing mediums. Nothing comes close to the internet when it comes to ease of collecting this critical data. We can actively track all traffic coming to your website and answer the following questions, and more: How did they arrive at your site? How long they were there? What did they do when they got to the site (and how much time did they spend doing it)? What products or services are getting the most attention? When people put things in their digital cart, what percentage of them will seal the deal and make a purchase? Even: What type of computer they were using? In short, not only can we accurately calculate the ROI of your various internet marketing strategies, but anything and everything you ever wondered about the effectiveness of your campaigns can be answered when the appropriate data is at your fingertips.

This type of data tracking is not available anywhere else in the marketing world. Needless to say, you can measure down to the penny how much you are making from your web presence. Think about any other marketing strategy you've used in the past, did you really know how effective it was? We can provide a real dollar-and-cents figure upon which you can rely when making future decisions about what type of marketing budget is appropriate for what period. If you already have a web presence, but don't track any of the data related to it, don't worry - ninety-nine percent of people we deal with don't track anything about the traffic to their website, so you shouldn't feel bad if you are part of that overwhelming majority. However, this is not an excuse not to start right away. Change is a gradual process, and we can help you start moving in the right direction. For some clients, basic tracking is all they need, which is a relatively simple process for us to implement. For others, advanced tracking may be desirable, and while this requires some customization, we can do that, too! The data tracking process is vital to any marketing campaign, and there is no medium where it is more achievable.

Return on Investment

Ignorance is not bliss when it comes to commerce. Pricing, customer care, **segmentation**,[16] and inventory management are all areas that can be improved upon by tracking data and calculating ROI. Big businesses are paying closer attention to **analytics**[17] and **big data**.[18] At first, no one knew what to do with such in-depth information, but they have been breaking new ground ever since they rolled up their sleeves and dove into the plethora of data flowing from internet data tracking. If you hesitate because you are uncertain of precisely what you would do with this new information, or frightened by what it might reveal about your business, you must keep in mind that your competitors are not hesitating; in fact, they are thriving *because* you are hesitating. You've left the field wide open for them, and, not only are they plucking all the low-hanging fruit, they have the whole orchard to themselves.

Analytics are nothing new. For example, early-bird specials are a result of basic analytics: during non-traditional dinner hours the demand at restaurants is lower, so restaurants lower their prices during non-peak hours

---

[16] Market segmentation is a marketing strategy that involves dividing a broad target market into subsets of consumers who have common needs and priorities, and then designing and implementing strategies to target them.

[17] "Analytics" simply refers to crunching tracking data to discover meaningful patterns in the data. The shift in levels of demand for airline tickets between weekdays and weekends described below is a meaningful pattern discovered from tracking data.

[18] "Big data" is an expansive term used to refer to collection of data sets that are so incredibly large and complex that they become difficult to process for identification of meaningful patterns.

in an attempt to increase customer demand at these times, and, ultimately, increase profits. But the availability of tracking data from the internet, and sophisticated computing technology, has taken analytics to a whole new level. Airline flights are cheaper on a Tuesday evening than they are on a Saturday morning. Why? Concisely, analytics show the demand is lower during the week. As the weekend comes, airlines jack their prices up in tandem until someone balks and the price will go no higher. Then, when peak demand has passed, prices roll back down through the early days of the week, and the airlines continue to maximize the prices can get for each ticket for another week. Data crunching – analytics - is what allows airlines to know whether their price is too high or too low at any given moment.

Data gives businesses a clearer view of what is going on with customers and/or operations. The best predictor of future behavior is past behavior. With the data in hand, businesses use **algorithms**[19] designed to interpret the data and establish optimal pricing, inventory levels, and investment strategies, or to eliminate any inefficiencies which have been identified. Implementing changes based on newly discovered inefficiencies in your business need not happen all at once in one dramatic upheaval. Your

---

[19] Algorithms are a set of rules built into a computer program, which is designed to perform a certain task. This sounds complicated, but it is often little more than a simple "If _____, then _____" function. In our airline example, the airline's ticket pricing program has an algorithm in it that basically says "If <u>demand is X</u>, then <u>increase/decrease ticket price to Y</u>." All the airline has to do is feed their tracking data (X) into the ticket pricing program, and the algorithm selects the best price (Y).

business has many moving parts, and there is absolutely no reason why you can't tackle them one at a time. Even small changes will create incremental improvements in your business, which will accrue over time and result in a dramatically streamlined business. The key is consistency. If you want to increase your bottom line, you must consistently strive to improve your understanding of your business and then act based on that improved understanding.

Don't go it alone, make sure you have the proper support before implementing change. Hire at least some people who are well-versed in reading analytics and data in some capacity. Know the data well enough to identify **micromarkets**.[20] Then, act on the new insight your data gives you by customizing your sales pitches to break into these micromarkets. The information is all out there. We can help you decode it and use it to your company's benefit. We very often find that micromarkets we identify for clients are not producing anywhere near their potential, but before we crunched the data our clients had no idea these micromarkets even existed. Big data can expand your existing business by identifying these types of opportunities. Just because you weren't able to really "break in" to a certain market or micromarket before doesn't mean it can't be done now. Allocate

---

[20] "Micromarkets" are narrowly-defined target audiences. Micromarkets are defined by a particular characteristic. For example, a lawn service might target micromarkets based on particular zip codes, neighborhoods, or customer types (i.e. residential, high net worth residential, low net worth residential, commercial, small businesses, or big businesses).

your marketing resources in a way that reflects the reality of the increasingly digital world we live in. Make a list of the top five things you believe your competition is doing and focus on the most-doable top three. They considered you in their marketing plan, now it is time to return the favor. Take the calculated risk.

Based on information gleaned from actively tracking data related to its business, a company can redeploy its sales force to exploit its growth potential. Sales territories should be updated often, as they are very often outdated. When the housing bubble burst, foreclosures across the country created dramatic changes in demographics nearly overnight. Change is always in the wind. Invest in your proven markets, but realize that **disruptive innovation**[21] is usually the single best route to take your business to the next level. Marketing costs are generally subject to intense scrutiny and are often the first thing on the chopping block when businesses tighten their belts, which makes it vital for marketing departments to show results, cut costs, and drive growth in real time. If you are uncertain about a proposed new course, make plays into **pilot markets**.[22] Evolution, be it

---

[21] Disruptive innovation is another expansive term; it is usually used to describe innovations that improve a product or service (or marketing strategy) in a way the market does not expect. In this context, we are using it to describe innovations that *you* had not expected. Examples of which might be as simple as developing proprietary web resources if you've never had them in the past, developing a customized data tracking package if you have proprietary web resources but are not making the most of them, or identifying and selling to a whole new market.
[22] A pilot market is a group (usually defined by geographic region or demographics) a business targets to test the viability of a product before doing a full scale roll out to a broader market.

measured or rapid, happens gradually, but a smart marketer knows they have to get out of their comfort zone by taking calculated risks. Tailor pitches to all customers, loyal and new.

It seems counterintuitive to invest more in tough economic times, but it's actually the best time to make money. Customers react to the economic squeeze by ensuring their scarce dollars are well spent by performing intense research before making any sort of purchase. Savvy business owners can take advantage of this period of heightened scrutiny by increasing their visibility, creating the content their customers seek (i.e., by supplying superb answers to their customers' questions and concerns), and increasing their market share. Every cent that goes into marketing should be an investment.

During the Great Depression Proctor and Gamble made a killing with Ivory Soap. During the greatest economic crisis of the past century Procter and Gamble began an annual competition for soap carving. Not only did this competition provide a wonderful distraction from the doom and gloom of the headlines, but it also sold tons of soap because there is no way to become a master carver without practicing on many a bar of soap. Needless to say, Ivory Soap sales thrived in the 1920s and '30s using this clever marketing strategy. There are always opportunities in the market place for ingenious marketers. However, your ROI depends on investing your marketing funds where they will deliver the most return. You should have a structured budget, but be flexible in fund allocation. Throwing money at a marketing problem is not enough; you need to understand what the money is doing to avoid waste.

The Final Frontier

Marketing based on big data has become an exact science. Marketers use data to understand consumers' buying responses to marketing strategies in both micro- and big-markets, which enables marketers to adjust their spending appropriately across each medium - from television to Twitter. The usual strategy is to examine actual sales over a period of time (a three-month period is a common sample size), as well as the intensity of activity changes from week to week. The big question for marketers is how to divide their focus between short- and long-term efforts.

A balance of short-term versus long-term must be struck, and efforts should be divided. Social media is ideal for short-term strategies. Unfortunately, the comparatively small amount of historical data makes forecasting results of long-term social media marketing strategies a bit more challenging. Social media does, however, have many benefits.

Social media can influence consumer brand choice. All products can take advantage of this phenomenon, even staples like dish soap (and staples). Social media, which is a lot like word-of-mouth marketing (but on a far higher order of magnitude) also lends itself to easy, automated data collection. We will go into greater depth on Twitter later on, but, in brief, the nature of this channel is that people make short posts (called "tweets")[23] related to anything their hearts desire. Tweets are often accompanied by topical keywords, and topics are said to be "trending" when a statistically significant number of twitter users are including a given topical keyword in their tweets. Something trending may be favorable or unfavorable to your business, as Twitter allows people to praise or badmouth businesses on an international scale. Because Twitter carries with it this inherent risk, and because a Twitter marketing campaign can be a train wreck in the wrong hands, businesses must exercise care not to tweet recklessly.

By way of example, the DiGiorno pizza company recently jumped aboard a trending topic on Twitter with disastrous results. The topic "#WhyIStayed" was trending, and, as DiGiorno has had relatively large amounts of success with encouraging people to forego going out to a restaurant in favor of a DiGiorno restaurant-quality pizza, DiGiorno jumped into the fray by tweeting that a DiGiorno pizza was the reason #WhyIStayed. Unfortunately for DiGiorno, the #WhyIStayed topic was

---

[23] Tweets are subject to a 140-character limitation, but users can add topical keywords above and beyond this limitation; topical keywords are easily identifiable because their first character is a hash tag. For example, a lawn service with a Twitter account might tweet, "Lawns R Us is loving this beautiful Sunday #LawnService #LawnsRUs." A Twitter user who is interested in lawn services might initiate a search using the topic keyword #LawnService, and Lawns R Us' tweet would be part of the search returns. A "trending" topic means that a statistically significant amount of Twitter users are posting tweets that contain that particular topical keyword in a certain time frame (i.e., #LawnService was trending on Monday, or #LawnService has been trending all week).

trending as part of a campaign to raise awareness for instances of domestic abuse in which the abused party is unable to extricate themselves from the abusive relationship for a variety of reasons (i.e., a person might tweet, "To protect my children #WhyIStayed"). Unsurprisingly, when DiGiorno suggested that a DiGiorno pizza was the reason #WhyIStayed, the Twittersphere lashed out violently against the company. This embarrassing situation could have been avoided with a modicum of research into the #WhyIStayed topic.

Big data won't solve all your problems, but it will provide new approaches and techniques to gain new insight into your business. A customer, either loyal or potential, is valuable. Your product or service can provide a solution to their problem in some manner, but you have to know them enough to personalize your approach. Personalization can easily yield a ten percent increase in sales. What are some ways to personalize? Ask yourself: What have they historically purchased? What sort of browsing or shopping do they do on their phone? Do they have a history of returning products or lodging complaints? Once you have a grasp on these individual nuances, set up marketing goals. Gaining insight into potential clients is not always easy, but it is always effective.

Gaining insight into effective practices neither comes easily nor freely. You must carefully consider and evaluate the various methods of engagement with potential customers to maximize your business' potential.

Big data won't solve all your problems, but it can help you decipher which times are optimal for engagement. For example, big data has demonstrated that tweets are almost useless after 3 p.m. on Fridays (because people aren't paying attention) and they do not regain their marketing value until Monday morning. Thusly, insights help you not to waste effort.

III. Realizing the Existence of the Web

Many of the points we address in this book come directly from the concerns of our clients. For example, our new clients are often puzzled by the relationship between the size and presence of their competitors' businesses in the real world versus the size of their presences on the web. Our clients will point out a competitor (often times a relative new-comer to the industry) and tell us the same three things: 1) this competitor's business always appear at or near the top of my search returns on Google; 2) I know this competitor has not done a substantial amount of business up to this point; and 3) this competitor is starting to get more and more business. When we hear this, we know we are really being asked a two-part question, namely: "Why is this relatively new business' website dominating my search returns, and how is this immature/unproven competitor attracting business over my well-established business?"

The answer usually lies primarily in the competitor's approach to marketing, which goes hand-in-hand with the quality of their web presence. The simple answer is that the competitor is a **digital native** – a person who grew up with the internet; a person to whom the internet is not a "technology" but a part of life as normal as having breakfast in the morning. A digital native needs no introduction to the value proposition of internet marketing, while the simple act of realizing the value of the web is a crucial first step that many **digital immigrants**[24] will never take. Digital natives voraciously embrace new technologies largely because the internet and rapidly evolving technology is all they have ever known, whereas digital immigrants are quite the opposite, having spent their formative years without the technology that is ubiquitous in our modern era. The comfort that digital natives feel with the internet is comparable to the comfort that digital immigrants feel with radio and television; different starting points on the timeline granted each group different perspectives about what is normal.

What we usually see is that the digital native builds his business around and through his web presence. His web presence is the primary focus of his efforts, while his brick-and-mortar location might be no more than a spartan garage (or non-existent). The digital immigrant, on the other hand, is usually on the other end of the spectrum: his focus is on his business' physical location and his proven track record of success. Based on these differing priorities, we already know who is going to put more effort into his web presence. Problematically for the digital immigrant, potential customers are increasingly using the internet as their primary research tool to determine what businesses to patronize. These potential customers evaluate businesses based on their web presences much in the same way a window-

---

[24] Anyone who did not grow up with the internet is a "digital immigrant." This is everyone except for the Millenials and the yet-to-be-named generation that is currently coming of age.

shopper walking down the street might determine that a given business is reputable based on the appearance of a business' brick-and-mortar location.

Here is a hard slap in the face about your competition: Your product or service may be superior, but if they do a better job marketing then no one will know it but you. To add insult to injury, your competitors are not even necessarily spending large amounts of time cultivating their web presence. If your competitors are well-informed as to the nature of internet marketing, twenty minutes per day is plenty of time for effective interaction through proprietary resources. For potential customers who use the internet for research, the only way they are going to find out that the well-established digital immigrant's business is superior to the newcomer's is if his web presence bears it out. A pristine, impressive brick-and-mortar location can be a valuable asset for use in an internet marketing campaign, but if the digital immigrant's website doesn't showcase his impressive brick-and-mortar location(s), or if his website fails to adequately demonstrate the size and scope of his business, potential customers are likely to skip right over the more reputable business for the newcomer's business with a better website. Remember, potential customers rarely know your business/industry as well as you do. So, they are less likely to know offhand how/why your business is superior to another, which makes things like price points and sleek websites determining factors for their decision making.

Another problem we commonly see with digital immigrants is that they have trouble visualizing what the internet really is – a vast market, with search engines operating as guides through the mayhem. To make matters worse, for many digital immigrants, the search engine is almost as incomprehensible as the steam engine was all those decades ago. If you fall into this boat and are having a hard time deciphering everything: Don't worry – we'll explain. To maximize your businesses' exposure in this incredibly vast market, it is important to know a few things about search engines.

Search engines are actually quite simple to understand. Search engines sort through an incomprehensibly large amount of information - which has been provided by business owners - to provide relevant links in response to a keyword-based query from a user. The user's keyword-based query is generally part of their effort so solve some sort of problem - the solution for which may be a website that sells goofy socks, or a website that describes how to get a red wine stain out of carpet. The search engine's response (i.e. the search returns, which includes links to businesses' websites, social media, and other facets of digital life) effectively presents the user with a market of businesses who may have a solution for the user's problem. The prominence of a websites' position in the search returns (i.e. being near the top of the page) has a positive correlation with the amount of traffic that reaches the website from that exact search. Thus, it pays to understand how search engines determine the order in which to display websites, and how to get your website at or near the top of those search returns.

The basic rules that affect the order websites will be displayed in a given search return are related to the length of time that the business has been visible in the marketplace and the relevance of the content on the website to the terms that were searched. However, the rules also allow for businesses to pay the search engines in exchange for a certain level of prominence in the search returns for certain keywords. Thus, the search returns contain relevant websites which are ordered by longevity and comparative relevance, with paid-for prominence guaranteed to any website willing to shell out the required fee. What search engines *don't do* is sort businesses based on revenues or reputation on the street. This is part of the reason why a well-established business does not necessarily come out on top of the search returns.

The paid-for prominence can be thought of like the business section of that tome of old: the Yellow Pages. Recall the Yellow Pages: many businesses appear, sorted by business type, as simple one-line text entries with a phone number next to them. Yet, others - those who have paid a fee - appear set off in large boxes with bold borders surrounding them. Just like in the Yellow Pages, many retailers choose to advertise with the search engine to have their business displayed more prominently in search results and to (hopefully) direct more people to their digital storefront. This advertising edge gives your business more visibility.

Realizing that search engines are a separate marketplace is vital to understanding the process of gaining visibility on, and revenue from, the web. Let's try a simple exercise to illustrate this:

Open up whatever device you use to browse. Go to Google and search for "blue nail polish." The search return is divided across two columns. The larger return on the left side of the screen lists different websites that Google has determined are relevant to your query (sometimes preceded by three to four paid advertisements). In the smaller column on the far right side of the screen are paid advertisements. These ads appear only because they were paid for; they are not meant to suggest any superiority of product or anything else. However, ask yourself this: If I was looking for blue nail polish, would my search extend beyond this first page, or would I be likely to click on one of the links on this first page? Internet marketing in general, and **search engine optimization**[25] ("SEO") specifically, seeks to capitalize on the tendency of consumers to visit (and patronize)

---

[25] Search engine optimization refers to the process through which the visibility of a website in a search engine's search returns can be affected. Search engine optimization takes into consideration the frequency of actual search terms people type into search engines and the way search engines work to maximize the visibility of a given website, which, in turn, drives website traffic.

websites that appear at or near the top of search returns from search engines.

Now, let's get back to the unanswered portion of the question we began this section with: Why would consumers choose a relatively new and unproven business over a well-established and reputable business? The answer is simple: Whether we like it or not, consumers are rarely the spitting image of rationality. In fact, consumers usually make *irrational* purchasing decisions based on incomplete information. Your website is your opportunity to present yourself as the end-all-be-all of your industry. Given the right web presence, potential customers are unlikely to even question whether a given company is the best in its area, they already know such is the case based on the impressive web presence they just browsed through and their goldfish-like attention span has already moved on.

Doubt that consumers are irrational? Think of any car commercial you've ever seen. These commercials focus on selling you a lifestyle associated with – not the specifications of – their car (if you think about it, we're sure you can come up with a multitude of industries where this rings true). Buy this Mercedes: you'll have beautiful friends and a glamorous life. Buy this gigantic Ram truck: you will join the ranks of the rugged-est of men with the power to tow a baseball stadium. Buy this Volvo: your family will be safe and happy. If you think companies with marketing budgets like major car manufacturers don't know what they're doing, you've got another thing coming. Successful marketing has always depended largely upon encouraging people to make their irrational spending decisions in a way that benefits some particular business.

Compete or Leave Business on the Table

"If you want to make money, go where the money is," Joe Kennedy famously declared. As a man who became a bootlegger to capitalize on the high demand and low supply of alcohol, he followed his own advice. Well, these days, people spend money on the internet, or use search engines to find places to spend their money. Nowadays, when we see or read about an intriguing product, business, or industry, we pull out our laptops (or smartphones) to find out more. Thus, even a television or print advertisement leads directly to the internet, where any information we could possibly want to know about a new product is only a few clicks away.

Your potential customers are so connected to the web that they have it is ingrained in their daily lives. Eighty-seven percent of adults have a cell phone. Twenty-nine percent of Americans look at their phones first thing in the morning and right before they go to sleep (which, coincidentally, are the times when the mind is both at its most fertile and most susceptible to suggestion). Almost half of us sleep with our phones on so we don't miss notifications. Technology is already a huge part of people's lives, and the demographics are only moving towards it becoming an even larger part.

It is crucial to have a strategy and long-term plan that includes an advertising budget (large or small) for internet marketing. A well-rounded online approach will pay you back in spades. Don't stop at just having a website. You need to maximize your website's visibility to potential clients through such channels as social media. In our modern age, there are more ways than ever to communicate with potential clients; it is silly to not take advantage of them. Think of each channel as yet another way to remind the greater public about your products/services. Advertise on television, but back it up with a great website for further research. As we've said before – the key to successful marketing is providing potential customers with multiple positive impressions of your business. Need another way to reach them? Twenty-five percent of people's time on the web is spent on social media – making it a necessary part of a well-rounded marketing approach. Successful businesses seek to enhance brand awareness then foster a positive relationship with potential, as well as loyal, clients. Deeper into the book, we will go more into depth about the various social media channels, but for now we'll give you a brief overview of a successful approach to internet marketing and burgeoning trends:

Based on the things we see people sharing on Facebook, we can draw some conclusions. For instance, people tend to post and share things like photos, jokes, links to interesting/funny articles, or news that they think will make them appear smart, funny, or even well-fed to their peers. While the fact that people are usually interested in enhancing their own appearance is hardly groundbreaking news, Facebook brought that fact (sometimes painfully) front and center, and it also created a brand new way for businesses to profit from this all-too-common trait. When businesses create share-worthy content their potential customers do the marketing for them. The big question is: How do I get people to share content related to *my* business? Well, profiting from social media has one golden rule: Content is king.

Developing share-worthy content is one of the cornerstones of any successful social media marketing campaign. Content that is interesting is more likely to be shared, so the focus should be on keeping your content fresh and interesting. In this fast-paced world, people don't want to have old ideas regurgitated to them ad nauseam; they want to learn something new. Additionally, Facebook has reminded us just how obsessed people are with enhancing their appearance - they want to appear smart, funny, or, at least, well fed. Moreover, people have learned that they can enhance their appearance by sharing things that are interesting, cool, or otherwise valuable. A business can capitalize on this desire to share by creating share-worthy content, which, in turn, increases the business' visibility through a process of instantaneous word-of-mouth marketing. Doing this consistently can lead to loyal followers who want to be the first to share the best content, and who will, in essence, do your marketing for you.

To stay on the share-worthy side of the line, content has to stay fresh You can't rely on last year's content to draw in new viewers. Madonna, if she has taught us anything of value, has taught us the value of reinvention. Every one of her albums had a new look and sound. In our opinion, this was critical to her success (honestly, we know it wasn't her voice). She kept people interested by constantly changing her look and thereby making herself an interesting point of conversation for decades. Keep the conversation going about your business by adding new content and features routinely.

Your approach to social media must be diversified today, tomorrow, and always. Thankfully, there are fairly obvious places to start: the three kings of social media are Facebook, Twitter, and LinkedIn. Every other site is secondary to them in terms of visibility. Once we have implemented a diversified marketing strategy that uses all three, we can use data tracking to determine which of them is the most efficient use of your marketing dollars, and then tailor the strategy to focus on that site while not ignoring the others. We want people to see your business everywhere they look. Remember, repeated exposure to a brand helps to build trust in that brand, and trust leads to conversions.

One of the many reasons Facebook, Twitter, and LinkedIn are so dominant is their emphasis on images. Popular websites intersperse images with their words to keep the reader interested. As discussed earlier, most people don't carefully read everything on the web – they scan it. Keeping this in mind, content must be pared down to deal with this phenomenon. Images help engage the reader and encourage them to continue reading. Another way to use images is through **infographics**,[26] which help explain ideas quickly and prevent the reader from being overwhelmed with information.

Finally, never forget that America is rapidly adapting to mobile-friendly websites. A website may look fantastic on a laptop or tablet, but a smartphone has different dimensions, which must be taken into account for maximum impact. Potential clients should not be inconvenienced in any way when browsing your site or they may become frustrated and move on to a better site. It is certain your competitors have already adapted. If you are not sure if your website translates on to a mobile device, check on your own devices for clarity. Make any changes necessary to make your business smartphone friendly.

SEO, PPC and Other Distracting Buzzwords

Not everything is rosy on the World Wide Web. Every industry has its downside. Unfortunately, when there is money to be made, there are hacks out there trying to prey on the uninformed. As a general rule, you must

---

[26] An infographic is simply a visual representation of information designed to convey data or information quickly. Think of your local weather channel, the map of the United States behind the weatherman, with different colors and numbers depicting different storm systems and temperatures around the country, is an infographic.

remember that there is no magical procedure by which some internet marketing companies can get you instant results where others cannot. The secret to success is in internet marketing is depth of research along with professional planning, implementation, and reporting. Accordingly, if someone promises to take you to the top of a certain Google ranking and they don't have some compelling facts that seem to back up that claim, take it with a grain of salt, and don't let some technical-sounding sales pitch overwhelm your skepticism. From what we've been told by clients, cold calls from internet marketing companies sound like this:

Cold Caller: *Ring, Ring, Ring*

Business Owner: Hello

Cold Caller: Hello, my name is Joe Smith from Miraculous Marketing. I noticed that your plumbing business website is not on the first page of Google for the keyword 'plumbing Miami.' You know that being 'found' on Google through **SEO** will be the foundation of your business moving forward.

Business Owner: Ok

Cold Caller: My Company Miraculous Marketing can get your website on the 1st page of Google within 4 months for a fee of $399/mo with a startup fee of $500.

Business Owner: What sort of work will you do to my website to get me on the first page of Google for 'plumbing Miami'?

Cold Caller: Our specialty is SEO. First, we will enhance the visibility of your website through a process called **on-site optimization**, and then we will send links to your site to push you up to the first page.

Business Owner: Umm... Ok. I don't really know what that means.

Cold Caller: Our business is technical. We will send reports explaining our work. No need to worry, we'll handle everything.

Many internet marketing companies rely on technical-sounding terms in an attempt disguise simple concepts as valuable information. The fact is, any internet marketing company worth its salt will be relying on SEO and on-site optimization to create more traffic for your website. The important part of this discussion is *how* the internet marketers are going to optimize your web site, and this is the part of the discussion that the hacks try to avoid having. In order to operate a profitable internet marketing business with fees of $399 a month, that internet marketing company would have to have hundreds of clients, and not very much staff. Internet marketing companies with bargain basement prices rely on a very high volume of clients – for whom they do relatively little – to stay afloat. Client retention is not a concern for these types of predatory internet marketing companies as long as there are enough uninformed business owners around (and we know there are).

Here's the ugly truth: creating successful proprietary resources online – ones that will create revenue for your business - takes time. A successful approach to internet marketing requires a sound strategy that combines in-depth research, paid advertising, and careful targeting of markets to generate organic traffic. Don't be fooled by companies offering instant gratification!

What Do You Need?

This is a great question for business owners to ask themselves (and one that we don't hear enough)! Necessity should be the primary driver of any marketing effort. Some of the best marketing initiatives come from a need to survive, expand, or nudge out the competition. However, sometimes the need is less obvious, and it is in these instances that a business owners' working knowledge of their business is vital to marketing strategy design.

The following is an example from a client of ours who sells and builds fabricated metal structures: Our client noticed that their buildings were being purchased by people and businesses for many different purposes. Our client's buildings were being used as horse barns, airplane hangars, storage facilities, and backyard sheds, but they were only marketed as plane old "fabricated metal structures." We all put our heads together, and devised a strategy to increase exposure in these various niche markets. Our client contracted to have several websites built, each of which touts the various benefits of using the same fabricated metal structures for each of the various purposes (i.e., he now has a website for fabricated metal airplane hangars, another for fabricated metal horse barns, etc.). The result? Our client is now perceived as an expert in building fabricated metal structures for each of the different purposes, and has increased his web-based sales for each category. As you can see, it was our client's particularized knowledge of his sales that allowed us to devise this strategy and reap the benefits of a thoughtful marketing strategy design process.

Unfortunately, the answer to this question varies for each of our clients, because every business has its unique challenges. For this reason, it is extremely important that business owners with particularized knowledge of their industry take part in marketing pushes. We often find this knowledge to help reach the tipping point for a successful campaign. There are steps we can take to improve our clients' web presence when they don't want to be involved in the process (i.e., they tell us "I just want you to handle this. Here's the money."), but the business/industry knowledge our clients bring to the table is simply irreplaceable.

Goals and Completing Them

Unless you are in Silicon Valley backed by Mark Zuckerberg and/or other celebrities, your chances of becoming an instant success on the web are almost nonexistent. More than likely, if you are reading this book you are a small business owner or marketing manager trying to make sense of the internet. You've heard stories of competitors moving mountains on the search engines and gaining market share from you.

As we've discussed, the first step is developing a strategy tailored to your needs. Needs-based determinations will also be informed by your goals for your business (Is your business a long-term venture? Are you a start-up looking to sell in 36 months?). Take a step back and try to visualize where your online business could be in six months, in nine months, and one year from now. From that standpoint, you can create a strategy and timeline to complete these goals. One of the best things about internet marketing is that it makes it easy to measure your progress towards your goals. We get a wealth of information about our clients' businesses in the form of black-and-white statistics. One of our colleagues likes to say, "If you treasure it, measure it," and we *treasure* consumer data. Contemporary digital marketing techniques allow interested website owners to gain invaluable insight into their businesses from their clients' perspectives.

Daily traffic levels are one such black-and-white statistic. The number of people who visited your site is indisputably and accurately traceable. Additional information we can glean is where traffic originated and what marketing effort caused it. Developing and optimizing content are both valuable marketing strategies, but the most powerful internet marketing campaigns' success is usually derived from word of mouth marketing (often through the medium of social media).

Word of Mouth Marketing

Word of mouth is the most potent form of marketing because people instinctively believe claims made by people they trust. We may, after some reflection, reject a claim, but, when someone we trust makes a claim, we initially give them the benefit of the doubt. For this reason, word of mouth marketing is priceless. Blasts from proprietary social media resources are a poor substitute for real-world word of mouth publicity for your business or product. Word of mouth publicity provides fertile grounds for creating and sustaining customers.

There are three types of customers: new, existing, and advocates. Marketers primarily focus on attracting new customers because getting new customers feels like they are moving forward. Chief Marketing Officers usually focus on acquiring new customers, creating a buzz for products, and raising brand awareness. However, sustaining customers through careful attention to customer satisfaction is the hallmark of successful commerce. Keep your existing customers happy! A lifelong customer is worth their weight in gold.

Moreover, everyone is a critic, but they can also be advocates. Contemplate the website Yelp.com. It is the democratization of public opinion. Businesses can't pay for - or change - these reviews. Once something is on there, it can't be permanently removed. Yelp's focus is on restaurants, which are businesses that present plenty of opportunities for individualized positive or negative experiences. Maybe the hostess got some bad news halfway through her shift and was short with a party, or the bartender was off on his measurements for someone's vodka martini. A customer might have a drink spilled on them through no fault of the restaurant, and still rip the restaurant apart online and vow to never return.

Customer opinion is important and, thanks to social media, immortal. No matter how badly you wish for your brand to be perceived in a certain way, customers have an annoying habit of making up their own minds. Word of mouth publicity is a potential end run of this habit. Potential customers will often rely on people they know to help them make up their minds. Word of mouth publicity gives your product the weight of that person's reputation, making it more credible. And, while people dislike being advertised to (seventy-six percent of people believe marketers are lying about their product in some way), they love sharing with each other. Treat your customers well and they will happily spread the word.

The types of businesses that benefit most from word of mouth marketing are those that are the best at what they do (or that have created the perception they are the best), provide a valuable experience, and reward loyalty is some fashion. Creating valuable experiences and rewarding loyalty can be as simple as remembering customers by their first name. Even if your business had a slip up, you can create a valuable experience for a customer by quickly correcting mistakes. Put your mind to it and come up with ways to reward your customers. Offer discounts, loyalty cards, "buy _, get _ free" offers, trial offers, hold previews, exclusive parties, or anything else you can think of. Customers are valuable and want to be treated as such. Make the effort to build loyalty. In the coming chapters we will discuss how to allocate your marketing budget, how to build an appropriate website, how and where to focus your social media efforts, and how to get the most out of the various search engines.

IV. Practical Budgeting - The Internet Is Not Easy Money

One of America's most popular sayings is that "there is no such thing as a free lunch in this world." We hear it all the time: nothing comes for free. Yet, we still hope one day the latest get-rich-quick scheme will make us overnight millionaires. However, when we are honest with ourselves, we know that there is no substitute for hard work. Learning things the hard way is our usual route to learning about ourselves and how to create practices that yield success. For example, most of us learned that scanning something we are supposed to know intimately is a recipe for disaster by the simple expedient of receiving a poor grade on an assignment during our schooling. Perhaps, in the wake of that failure, you discovered you were a visual learner, made yourself flash cards, and earned a grade you were satisfied with on a subsequent assignment or examination. The end result was that you learned something about yourself and what works best for you. In business, as in life, we build on our experiences.

In the same vein, a successful internet marketing campaign is not conceived and implemented overnight. In many respects, it is a marathon rather than a sprint. Success is a result of perseverance and effort over time. Many people fantasize about escaping the rat race by building a successful business that relies on revenues from the internet. What must be understood is that, like any quality business, successfully generating revenues from the internet requires commitment and responsibility. Part of that obligation is being realistic about what to expect. The idea of setting your own hours is enticing, but the reality is you may have to work around the clock to make sure all tasks are completed. With your own business, there is no clocking out.

Your budgeting should emphasize that the most important people in your business are the customers, not the investors. If customers are responding to a marketing campaign, go with it. Your goal is to accrue (and then keep) customers and they know their needs better than anyone else. One of the best ways to make it plain to customers that your business, service, or product can fulfill their needs is to keep your approach simple. In response to some praise he received after writing a rather terse letter, Mark Twain stated, "If I had more time, I would have written a shorter letter." When in doubt simplify and then re-simplify. Your customers, no matter what your business is, will respond to your de-complication of their lives. Focus on their pain point and resolve it in a way that exceeds their expectations.

Businesses should go through a planning stage before being launched. Would-be entrepreneurs should carefully consider what they are offering, to whom they are making an offer, and for what price. A strategy and a plan must be developed and then put into action. Unfortunately, no matter how amazing your product or service is, people are usually not going to be waiting next to their computer for your website to launch. Your potential customers are busy living their own lives and trying to filter out good information from bad information. Your success depends on your ability to differentiate your product or service as one that makes people's lives easier, and to make it stand out from your competitors'. Success doesn't usually happen overnight, and a rational entrepreneur shouldn't expect it to. Success should revolve around the implementation of a carefully thought out plan, and then continuously refining that plan with small, incremental improvements based on experiences.

Setting a reasonable budget is key to a successful internet marketing campaign. Most small businesses spend either too much or too little. Ideas can't be tested in a vacuum, so be careful that all parts are integrated and are allocated the best amount to function. Your plan should encompass at least a twelve-month period and account for low points during periods when people usually vacation (such as August and certain holidays). Do not waste time and money as you will not get either back.

Getting the word out about your business or product should be an incremental process. Companies set themselves up for failure when they seek instant gratification by hiring a pricey public relations company to create a marketing blitz on behalf of their product or service. Word of mouth is one of the most powerful marketing tools, but seeing results from word of mouth marketing requires time. Your products won't sell themselves. Basing your future success on your past success does not pay the bills. In marketing if you aren't trying, you are dying!

Calculating your internet marketing budget should begin with a self-evaluation of several factors, including:

- What type of industry are you in?
- Taking into account the size of your business and the rate of growth of your industry, are your goals realistic when compared with industry benchmarks?
- What are you spending on internet marketing now?
- How frequently are you spending?
- What have your results been to date?
- Who is your target audience and what is the best way to approach them?
- What are your one-time expenses?
- What are your ongoing expenses?

Also keep in mind that that appropriate levels of marketing spending vary across businesses. Retail businesses spend more than educational businesses. Small business are exceptionally different than large corporations. One rule we have heard is that, if it can, a business should spend seven to eight percent of its revenues towards marketing efforts. While this represents a significant expense, failing to allocate sufficient funds to marketing can be far costlier. You must spend time and money to spread the word about your product or service on every available medium of communication. It is this "spreading the word" that develops your brand.

Allowing people to easily find information about your business is the key to creating the positive impressions that lead to converting people into customers. Marketing should be a top priority and not the last consideration to get any leftovers. Allocate enough money to do a proper job marketing. What you allocate is up to you, but think about it this way: a few more dollars in the marketing budget could determine whether or not your business succeeds. You should have two types of marketing expenses: one-time expenses and ongoing expenses. Getting business cards printed or launching a website should be a one-time expense. Running ads on search engines and websites related to your industry are ongoing expenses. With the knowledge of the difference, budget wisely. Properly identifying the nature of an expense is important to creating a realistic budget.

As soon as your plan has a budget and timeframe, develop the right kind of attitude towards it. You should be flexible with your plan, and you should reject anyone selling a one-size-fits-all mentality (just because someone you know may have had positive results from advertising through LinkedIn does not mean you should devote your entire budget to LinkedIn advertising). Every single business is different. Don't allow yourself to develop a one-track mind; read as many advice articles as you can handle and constantly challenge yourself to learn more. In marketing, there are no prizes for stubbornness. Markets change constantly; what was true last year or even weeks may not hold true today. Revisit your marketing approach regularly, but especially when launching a new product or service.

Not Easy Money – Earned Money

It is easy to think that the web is easy money, but it is not the case. The web provides the *potential* to reach a massive audience, but you have to advertise effectively to reach that audience and then convert them to sales. As stated repeatedly in this book, consumers must see your brand several times before even considering a purchase. Effective advertising depends in large part upon creating positive impressions of your brand for potential customers, which is how you build your brand's reputation. For this reason, the longer a business has been advertising on the web, the farther along it has the potential to be in the brand-building process. Put simply, those brands which pioneered internet marketing have a stronger record of impressions. Getting money from the web is an old-fashioned process – you must earn it.

Like we said, content is king, and having an existing portfolio of content is another benefit that comes from the longevity of your internet marketing effort. Updating content is far easier for a company with a large portfolio of content. It takes a comparatively massive amount of work to put together great content from scratch. But don't let this make you feel defeated right out of the gate; every business has to start somewhere. Businesses become successful at internet marketing by putting in the work to methodically reach the goals they set for themselves. This is a process that requires careful attention to determine where the business is making gains and suffering losses so that the business can be optimized. Successful businesses don't just hire a marketing team and then call it a day.

Practice makes perfect in all walks of life. Companies who were internet marketing pioneers are experienced in the web. Their money was not made overnight. Make a plan, execute it, and work hard to achieve your own success. There are no exceptions to this rule. Forget the stories you heard about the internet being easy money – they are urban legends.

Growth: Advertising vs. Organic

Here is something no one will tell you, especially internet marketers: even without ongoing SEO, your traffic from search engines will grow all by itself (we call this "growing organically" or "organic growth"). Because of this, one of the most talked about subjects between clients and the marketers they hire, and between marketers, is: whether it is best to rely upon paid advertising or organic growth to increase traffic from search engines?

The short answer is that it depends. Paid advertising makes a lot of sense for many industries. For example, if your product has a profit margin above $50 (which probably means your price point is above $100), it may make sense to pay as much as $20 per sale for paid advertising, as that would still allow you to make $30 on each online sale. However, if your product has a low price point (in the $2 to $6 range, for example) and small margins, it is far more difficult to earn a profit when using paid advertising. Additionally, some industries are prohibited from using paid ads (for example, if your company sells tobacco or e-cigarette products). For these reasons, some companies are limited to organically growing traffic from search engines.

If your company provides a service, as opposed to selling a product, the answer is more complicated. You have to determine the lifetime value of a customer, which is difficult in the best of times. Even the most enlightened marketing savant has a hard time putting a price on the value of selling a one-time service to a client and quantifying what that one customer is worth long term. A clear answer depends on the business you are in and the goals you have for your marketing dollars. Our recommendation is to always have a well-rounded online campaign that invests in, and is focused on, creating long-term relationships with customers. The lifetime value of a customer is well worth the investment now. Every business owner can tell you off the top of their head who are their best customers by first name.

Your marketing dollars should be spent with the idea of finding more lifetime customers and clients.

The Myth of "Launch and Thrive"

When you launch a website, the first month can be exciting. You are putting your "Open for Business" sign into the digital world, and seeing your logo pop up in a Google search return is an inexplicable delight. The thrill usually lasts about a month until you realize there hasn't been much business. Next comes what we refer to as the "winter of our digital discontent." You can usually count on at least six months of inactivity on your newly minted website if it has not been optimized for visibility on search engines. During this period, people may stumble upon your site organically through a keyword search, but those people will be few and far between. Remember, it is a busy world on the internet. Don't be discouraged by periods of slow growth. This time period is truly a testing ground for those who are serious about their businesses. What happens when results are not immediately forthcoming is a true test of commitment. This is the time that we actively track the traffic data coming from your site and take steps to increase that traffic. Stay the course through this period you will see results (quality results usually take between one and three years to materialize). Not quick enough for you? Sorry, there are no shortcuts.

The idea of "launch and thrive" comes from two places: urban legends and predatory practices by website developers. To real internet marketers, the idea is an abomination. <u>Launching a website does not mean that you will make money from the website</u>. The truth of it is that the internet is a competitive place, just as competitive (or more so) than the business world itself. If it was as simple as launching a website and the money just started to pour in, there would be many more internet millionaires out there than there are (even allowing for inflated claims of success).

Websites are internet storefronts, while you may see some traffic from the occasional passerby during the early days of your launch, the ultimate success of your website, like any business, flows from the decisions you make to market and create revenue from your site. Moreover, search engines do not "trust" new websites. The first and most important job that search engines perform is to eliminate websites with fraudulent content from their search results. To that end, search engines filter out many brand new sites simply because new sites have a higher probability of being fraudulent sites.

The search returns from Google, Yahoo and Bing's **organic listings**[27] operate off an algorithm that scans websites for content. What does this

---

[27] "Organic listings" refers to the part of your search returns that appeared because a website has content that was relevant to your search, and not just because the website paid for prominence in searches for that specific keyword

mean? Every couple of weeks, a search engine program will scan your site for new content and other aspects of your site. They do this to use your information to make money from their paid advertisements. When the program has run through a site fifty times and sees the same website aspects for a few years, the search engine shifts that website from the "new and fraudulent" category to the "trusted" category. It is that simple.

Traffic Isn't Always the #1 Goal!

Let's get this straight from the start - traffic is almost always a good thing. This section is meant to take a step outside of the rat race for traffic that consumes internet marketers and business owners alike. Consistent traffic is a symptom of bigger sales/leads to come. However, ignoring what you are doing with the visitors coming to your website is costly. We can't stress how important it is to engage your visitors using your knowledge of your business.

The soul of all marketing is language. Getting people to notice your brand through the use of language is the foundation for spreading your brand. Having great language content is paramount to converting visitors to customers. We like to stress to our clients how important their content is. Too often business owners get caught up in the many distracting tasks of building a website. While logos, pictures, and background colors are all important (and deserving of attention), content can make or break a potential client. Grabbing the visitor with the first few words or paragraphs on your webpage is your best chance at success.

The Importance of Branding

Branding is a continuous battle. Building a brand is one of the more difficult tasks in growing a business. When a brand is recognizable there is a certain trust that goes with it. What does the consumer trust? That the company has the money to advertise enough that you saw the brand all over the place. There is validity in that. A company that has the budget to advertise is one of two things: A well-planned and funded start-up or a successful business.

On the web, branding is even more important. Branding is what allows companies to convert search traffic to **brand traffic**.[28] For example of this conversion, think of a visitor who arrives at a site through a Yahoo search for "baby pacifier," and then returns to the site a week later (skipping the search engine) to make a further purchase. This simple process is the fundamental goal of any marketing initiative online. For customers to surf the abyss of companies on the internet, find yours and remember the site is the ultimate goal. In general, customers will visit a site multiple times

---

[28] Brand traffic refers to visitors who arrived at your page by not only typing in a search keyword, but also by using your business name as a keyword. For example, if someone arrives at Ace Hardware's website by searching "ace hardware store" in Google; rather than searching "hardware store."

before making a purchase or contacting the business. Make those visits count!

Branding is not simple either. Having a great website, in the realm of the internet, is not enough. A solid company now has a great website, a wealth of social media followers, and some form of online paid advertising. These proprietary resources are the company's online platform for reaching out and ultimately branding on the internet. Anyone who follows the analytics of a site with ecommerce tracking will tell you that customers go from search engines, to a brand's Facebook page, to a brand's website, back to the Facebook Page, and through many other websites before making a purchase. A solid branding platform online is vital for success through search engines.

V. WEB SITES

Think about the last time you drove by a billboard that caught your eye. Maybe it was an ad for ambulance chaser or a watch ad with David Beckham. Everyone from the graphics designer to the idea guy for the ad has now done their job: they got your attention! Unfortunately, it is very difficult for the company that sponsored the ad to track their return on investment from billboard advertising. Maybe you picked up your phone and called the number on the ad right away to speak to that lawyer or ask about the watches. Did you mention the ad? When marketing data falls through the cracks because a business forgets to ask, or the customer fails to mention, where the customer heard of the business, we refer to it as **leakage.**

Leakage is almost non-existent for internet marketing. Everything is traceable and the software is only getting better. We can even track what your website visitors do with their mouse while they are browsing your site. Think of the advantage this gives you in the internet marketing context: Whereas a billboard is placed at a location and does not change until it comes down, internet marketers can actively change their pages to fit the behavior patterns of the visitors. For example, if the mouse movement shows a draw toward an area of the page that is empty, a clever marketer can move a **call-to-action**[29] into that area to make the page more likely to convert visitors to sales. Not only can you benefit from data collection from the moment your site goes live to the moment you take it down, but, once your website is indexed by search engines, your website will exist in the search library forever. Additionally, as we mentioned before, your website organically gains trust from search engines over time, which creates a self-reinforcing cycle where your website is promoted more highly in the organic listings, which causes more traffic to flow to your site, which causes you to be promoted more highly in the organic listings.

First impressions count, and, while we can't gauge opinion, we can measure the effect of your first impressions! This data point is your **Click Through Rate** ("CTR"). The formula for CTR is simple: clicks/impressions (the number of times your ad is clicked divided by the number of times the ad was shown). If an ad is shown one hundred times, and it is only clicked once, then its CTR is one percent. Your CTR affects the **quality score**[30] of your website, which, in turn, affects your visibility. There is no one size fits all approach to maximizing your CTR. Every campaign is different, as is the

---

[29] A call-to-action attempts to induce a visitor to engage in a particular action. For example, at the end of a short article explaining the value proposition behind using a fabricated metal structure as a grain silo, a website may have a large button that says "Order Yours Now!" That button is the call-to-action.

[30] Search engines calculate a quality score for each website that is indexed, a website's quality score is a big part of how search engines determine the order in which ads are listed. Quality score is determined in part by click through rate, ad copy relevance, landing page quality, landing page load time, and other factors (the exact formula has not been revealed by the major search engines).

competition in the search returns for each keyword. Don't be afraid to tailor your approach, you will earn stronger yields. The choices you make with respect to which keywords to focus your advertising efforts on must be carefully thought out because you usually have to pay for every click. If your website misleads visitors to increase traffic in the hopes that visitors will stick around to check out your product, you will lose leads and consumer trust, which will negatively affect your **bounce rate.**[31] Your website should focus on keywords that are relevant and affordable. Not every keyword is the same.

Getting a Useful Website

One of our favorite comparisons to building a website is building a house. Just like the famous Tom Hanks movie 'Money Pit', a website can pull apart your bank account and stress your life out. Along the same lines, the reasons for why a house-build goes awry are the same reasons a website development project goes wrong. Here they are in the simplest of forms:

- Inexperienced contractor
- Poor blueprints
- Cheap materials (software)
- Indecision

---

[31] Bounce rate is a measurement used in web traffic analysis. Expressed as a percentage, your bounce rate tells you how many visits to your website end on the first page the visitor sees (without viewing other pages within the site).

- Insufficient Funding

Just like millions of homes have been built and millions of websites have been built successfully, there is a good way to go about it and a bad way. We will explore both methods in this section and hopefully give the reader a few guidelines how to create a great looking, engaging website for their target demographic.

Here is the ugly truth; perhaps the "beautiful rule" would be a better description. Your site can look great and have zero positive results for your business. A site must be *functional* in the eyes of the search engines and the user to be most effective. If your brand is so popular that consumer's flock to you, your business may be able to survive off your magnificent brand recognition, but you should still format your site so that Google, Yahoo and Bing can read your content effortlessly. Even with a healthy amount of traffic, websites depend upon smooth site navigation and seamless operational ability to convert visitors to customers. We refer to websites that have these traits as user-friendly websites.

Make sure your site is user-friendly. If you have a high bounce rate, you might want to review the logistics of your site. Ask yourself objectively if a warm lead will find a solution to their problem quickly and easily on your page. Do not scrimp on site design, your competitors invested money on their websites to create a "wow" factor, if your site looks cheap and is not user-friendly it will come across as spam. Be truthful in what you offer, don't attempt to mislead potential clients-it never works. Set expectations appropriately and state your motivations in the friendliest manner possible. Make sure you have authority, but don't sound bossy. Offer choice not obligation. Be interested in your client's experience. Write in plain English, no one likes being talked to over their head.

Be search engine friendly, too. For example, search engines cannot "read" (i.e. index) Flash sites. What this means is that your Flash website is effectively invisible to search engines. Moreover, Flash sites are not supported by mobile phones. Mobile phones are such a big part of digital marketing now; not having a site that can be comprehended on a mobile phone is a death sentence on the web.

Another element of user-friendliness relates to site design – how should you use pictures, text, and other rich media content? Where is the best place for it on the home page? These are great questions and the answer depends on a multitude of factors. For one, the industry you are in is important, consumers looking for an accountant are anticipating a different look and feel to a website than a consumer looking for a bathing suit. Not to mention, their preconceptions will have a lot to do with whether they purchase or reach out for the services offered. Generally, images are better to grab attention while rich content will assist in providing the details or the incentive to take the next step in purchasing or calling.

Ensure that your text is clear and does not fall victim to odd interpretations. Bad grammar can negatively affect your credibility. Any appearance of a lack of professionalism may cause your potential customer to move on to a competitor. The form header at the top of your page should be direct and deal with the pain points your visitors are seeking to alleviate. Get rid of fluff, but engage the visitor toward your desired call-to-action. Your call-to-action should be designed first, because it is important to have a clear picture of where you want your site to drive your visitors. If you have a video, state the purpose. Your headline, - what is on top of the page drawing viewers in - subhead (the secondary headline), and introductory paragraph should represent your unique value proposition. Ask for an email over a phone number. Some are still smarting over the telemarketing craze of the past, particularly digital immigrants, and are leery of giving out their numbers.

Infographics are generally about stats, but help break up text to avoid boredom. If you are going to spice things up by adding a video, keep in mind you have to assume people will not watch the video. Your copy should be able to be read in isolation and still make sense. Most scan, but some may take the time to read and everything must stand alone. Make testimonials believable. A cupcake site will probably not win any points with its target audience for having Hell's Angels as endorsers. Minor details are also important, for example, your testimonials should be kept current (as opposed to having a testimonial dated from 2011, why not have a current one). Show, don't tell, what you offer and speak with authority.

A **landing page** is one a warm lead can land on to move to the next step of the buying cycle. It can link to your website, but is designed to stand alone for a singular purpose. It is almost pushy in nature and a business uses them to grab clients and not let them get involved with navigating your site. There are two types of landing pages: click through and lead generation.

Click Through and Lead Generation

Elegant and focused should be the direction for your landing page. This is a concise call to action and everything on this single page should support that. Information should be used to direct this goal and some appealing visuals should also be included. Even though most visitors abhor pop-ups, this page should include a pop-up which asks visitors who are leaving the site prematurely if they will leave their information with you for a follow-up. Additionally, your landing page might have an option to live chat with a customer service or sales representative, which demonstrates the company's commitment to customers at every step of the buying cycle. While pop-ups can be annoying, in certain scenarios they have relatively high conversion rates, and your bottom line should be of more concern to you than a slight annoyance.

The **hero shot**[32] on your landing page should be prominent as it gives leads a visual to focus upon as they search for solutions. Words are also key. Communicate about the offering and don't just throw out buzzwords. Scanable headlines should be used to tell any backstory. Whatever the color of the page, put your call-to-action in a hue that will catch the eye. Calls-to-action should be descriptive and explain the benefits. Include whitespace and do not try to cram as many visuals as possible. The viewer should not get a headache from looking at your site. In addition, limit the benefits you are providing to three bullets, and get to the point early – don't leave the best information for the end of the page. If the viewer has to ask why they should sign up, you have already lost them, especially if you are using squeeze tactics (otherwise known as creating a false sense of immediacy). Trying to say availability is limited comes across as desperate. Name the price before you give a percentage off. Show the original price before giving a discount. Enticing the customer with the promise of a discount before giving them the information necessary to evaluate the discount is tedious and confusing. Target and segment your viewers. If you try to appeal to everyone, no one will be satisfied.

When a lead visits your page the goal should be gathering information. Providing a call-to-action that requests information is one way of gathering

---

[32] A hero shot is a visual representation (a picture or video) of the product or service you are offering which demonstrates your product or service in use, so that visitors can see the benefits of your product or service.

additional information. This form should be singular and short. No one loves filling out forms and many find them tedious. Make sure your font size is appropriate as small bullets are too much of a bother to read. Some words are turn offs and should be avoided. Do not repeat information as it is only one page. Set the expectation of the form. If you are going to call them back, then do so. If there is no way to do this, ask for emails. A drop down form helps them get specific about what they want fixed. Make the desired result of your call-to-action clear, creating high expectations and failing to meet them is a recipe for disaster.

How Much to Pay for a Website

This is a great topic for discussion. Right off the bat, we can tell you that we have NEVER seen a website with an attractive level of design and operational functionality for under $1,000 (this, of course, excludes family and friends of web designers and marketers who have received a hefty discount). Any web developer who offers you a website for less than this figure is not putting enough work into the development, branding, content, images, and optimization of the site. Here is a great general rule:

A quality website for a small business owner should be in the neighborhood of two to three thousand dollars.

There are many aspects that affect the pricing of a website. Will the website be dedicated to e-commerce or lead generation? How large is the website in actual pages? These are questions that you should at least have a rough answer for *before* you start searching for a company to build the site for you.

What makes a site expensive or not is the customization. The actual layout of the site is either a previously built template or a custom template. To determine whether your template was custom built for you, ask to see the **wireframe**, which is essentially a rough blueprint of what your site will look like. With the wireframe in hand, peruse the company's portfolio of work and keep an eye out for websites that have identical layouts. This basic level of scrutiny will help to keep your company from being taken advantage of. When in doubt do research and ask questions.

Where Do Visitors Come from?

This is a topic that keeps radio sales executives awake at nights. How do you report success or failure to your customers that purchase spots on your radio, newspaper, or billboard? You have to hand it to them; it is not for lack of trying that they have failed at this endeavor. You hear it all the time, "tell the person at the counter that Wild Bill Moore sent you and receive a 10% discount!" That 10% discount is a hit the store is willing to take to see if their marketing efforts are worth it. Another is "cut out this coupon and take it with you for a 15% discount." These discounts amount to advertisers having to pay twice for their advertising just so they can have a shot at calculating their ROI. The digital world is exactly the opposite. Rather than struggling to accumulate data, our issues are related to winnowing down the data to draw meaningful conclusions. Everything is traceable!

When we are talking with new clients, we are often asked, "Why aren't customers contacting me through my website?" Usually, we have to ask a question of our own in order to provide a meaningful response, "How long has your site been live?" From here, the conversation goes in one of two directions. The first, and the more likely, is that they just launched the site, but spent very little on its design and search engine optimization. If this is the case, the answer to the question is easy - whether it is on the internet or a retail location, new brands are not trusted! The second, when the site has been up for a while and they are still not getting any action from the internet, is less common and more complicated. The answer in this case usually relates to a lack of **on-site optimization**,[33] which could be a result of a poorly-researched optimization effort, a failure to identify appropriate targeted keywords, or, in the worst case scenario, an industry that is dominated by a website giant.

The visitors to your site come from where you decide to market yourself on the search engines. There are few surprises when it comes to

---

[33] On-site optimization refers to the process of making your website more attractive to search engines through inclusion of relevant content, keywords, and increasing keyword density.

traffic online. Nearly all traffic is triggered by some form of marketing initiative. For example, a press release that is picked up by a local newspaper can spurn a decent return in referral traffic from that local media outlet. Internet traffic is very much in the realm of cause and effect!

Modern Sharing Model

No man is an island. Every business is accessible as long as they are using the web. The internet was born out of the idea of sharing information. Google very much cares what other people think of your site. They want to provide search returns that include sites of significance, which is a hallmark of value for the search engine. Your content should be marked for authority and value to move up on the search engine ranks. Higher rank =more traffic. Some effort should be made to share trustworthy, reciprocal links with other websites ("sharing links" means that you put a link to another businesses' site on your page, and vice-versa). For example, a restaurant may consider linking with a silverware distributor and a farmer's market. However, two competing Italian restaurants should not share links. Guest blogging is another way to build links. That process looks like this: The guest blogger, preferably a reputable person, makes a post for your website. You provide a link on your website to the guest blogger's website, and he provides a link on his website to his content on yours. The end result is that both parties benefit by sharing in each other's traffic.

It is a compliment when someone wants to put your link on their site and vice versa. But you must be careful with this, sometimes people have hidden agendas or websites have questionable content. If there is a chance that someone might be offended by the site, do not link to it. In America being offended is some people's hobby. Go through a site carefully before allowing a link - common sense is not so common.

Another avenue is to write a press release for an event you are hosting. Maybe you have a specialty teashop and want to create a buzz for a new type of Chai through hosting an unveiling of an exclusive brand. Someone is bound to be interested enough to spread the word resulting in traffic and links. But remember, link sharing can be dangerous. Don't link to questionable sites. Links come through directory listings, reciprocal links, and paid links and it was once beneficial to have them on your site as they helped in organic search results by bolstering your presence. Being in a directory can help you create a niche market.

Another way to increase links is by repackaging your content. Throw in some graphics and repost the same content, or just have someone read it for a YouTube video. There are many ways reinvent your writing. In addition, any time your company name is being used for an event, pick up links. If you are sponsoring a workshop or hosting a conference gather as many reputable links as possible. Events usually have more than one and they benefit from picking up some reputable links as well. Cross-referencing is a solid way to earn links. If you are at a conference, try to network and build your professional reputation with quality links. Directories are a great source for link building as long as you go for quality over quantity. Local directories are a good source of geographic traffic and links, professional directories and online ones like LinkedIn are great for reference building. The best directories are ones for your field. Always aim for quality over quantity.

Google has recently been cracking down on paid links. A paid link is when money is exchanged to bring leads to your website. Google was receptive to them in the beginning, but now penalizes websites for using them. Google has many rules regarding paid links that may contradict each other, so it is just best to steer clear. And, a competitor would be well within their rights to report you.

Olive Branches and Arms – When to Collaborate and When to Destroy

One of the worst things you can do in business is to badmouth your competition. If someone leaves a negative review of your business, then the best way to handle it is to confront the problem head on. Do not waste time feeling victimized or defensive. Address the problem in the same forum it was presented. Being public shows you have nothing to hide. Everything and everyone will always have a dissenter. The solution is not to have people like you, but to deal with vocal opponents gracefully. If a person is completely unreasonable, take as many steps as possible to ameliorate the situation.

When addressing the problem, make sure you have a reasonable solution. If someone complains about a food item, comp them a meal. If you are a florist shop and the calla lilies were wilted, offer a free bouquet. Treat this negative feedback as a valuable opportunity to show off your customer service.

The web has promoted information sharing since the beginning. However, you do not want to give away so much information that all your cards on the table. Know when to share and when to compete. Given the vastness of the internet, everything can be found about everything. Trade secrets are not so exclusive anymore. Some marketers are more than willing to give away information to score more traffic. It works in the short-term, but not necessarily in the long term.

Any information you publish in the web is fair game for your competitors. If you change the design of your website or offer specials, they have the right to borrow your ideas until they make them their own. If at any point you think to yourself that this is not fair, realize that being unfair is not illegal.

The best way to annihilate your competitor is to know them as much as possible. Browse their online information. They are putting it out there so it is fair game. Look at your competition's landing page, price points, and the like. What type of tweets do they send out? Did they create a Facebook page? How do they interact with their clients in a public forum? All these questions can be answered in a few minute's time, just do the research.

If you find their website is more intriguing than yours then take notes as to why. Maybe their website is well-designed and their content is solid. You should study their content more than design as any overly flashy website comes off as desperate. Most people don't enjoy being advertised to. By making it as pleasant an experience as possible you give yourself an edge over the competition. Ask others their opinion of your website and take their feedback seriously. It is easy to dismiss someone's opinion if it does not match yours, but unless you ask a surly teenage who hates everything, there is value in all forms of feedback. Separate the chafe comments such as "I like your color scheme" from the true nuggets. For example if someone thinks your call-to-action is too confusing, then understand that it probably is. Visitors to your site cannot read your mind and this feedback is invaluable for making sure you are making everything as easy as possible for potential leads.

Interact as much as possible with your advocates. If a blogger is raving about your product/service, send them a thank you card, ask for their feedback, or send them a free product or coupon. When you demonstrate to people that you are listening, they will champion your business. Don't take it for granted when people like your business – reward them and make them *love* it.

A/B Testing

A/B testing (read: A or B testing) pits two or more design pages against each other to see which works best with the targeted audience. The goal of a/b testing is to gather data and gain insights related to your content, graphics, media, etc. Getting insight is the only thing that matters, without it even the prettiest landing page is worthless. Your personal preferences do not matter. Your ego cannot take the wheel of your business. Start with a hypothesis about your page to get the ball rolling. Anything is worthy of testing as long as you have a metric and something to start with. Keeps yourself focused on gaining insight and do not make unnecessary changes.

Customer feedback is great for a/b testing. Make giving feedback easy and rewarding. But take heed, feedback only has value if testers feel comfortable even to disagree with you. Dictators surround themselves with yes men and put to death any dissenters. Don't lose touch with reality by alienating those who might disagree with you. The most valuable opinions are those that challenge something you hold to be true. You are serving your customers well if they feel that they may be rewarded for, or at least are comfortable with, being contrary.

Things to consider when assessing your direction and content

Who is your audience? Take the time to really focus on this portion of targeting and segmenting.

Where do they live?

Why are they seeking out my products and service?

What value do I hold for them?

Am I offering enough or too much?

What makes them agree or disagree with me?

Am I offering a clear-cut focus?

How can I address any objections they may have?

What should be added or removed for maximum impact?

What do my prospects need to know in order to say yes?

Set Goals

Setting goals for your website is like any projection: try to be conservative in your estimates. Here is an example for a site-selling pacifiers:

Jan.1- Site Launch

Mar. 1- 15 visits/day

June 1- 25 visits/day

Sept 1- 40 visits/day

Dec. 31- 60 visits/day

This would be strictly organic visits from search engines. Organic growth is a necessity for a successful initiative online. It takes time to produce results from the organic listings online, a year may seem like a long time, but not if you look at it from the right vantage point. Most businesses that are getting started would love to flourish within a year.

You can convert leads if the viewer can trust you. The truth is consumers do not trust advertising, but they should trust you. You may not be able to buy trust, but you can build it. Give visitors as much information as they want. Perhaps allow the option of downloading an eBook that is of substance. Offer resources throughout the buying cycle. Check your information and grammar with a fine toothed comb. If you are selling one thing, don't distract the visitor with information about something else, or use corny phrases such as "act now." At this point, people are tired of marketing efforts that create a false sense of immediacy. It is better just to state the information rather than emit rallying cries.

Corey Consulting can track phone calls, track sales in an ecommerce site, and most importantly create reports to find trends. The end game here is that we can justifiably say that we succeeded or failed in our initiatives. The days of "I think that marketing campaign worked" are over and the new age of **black/white marketing**[34] is here to stay. Efforts either succeed or they do not. These data points allow a business to take action with clarity and vision, more so than ever before.

---

[34] Marketing with clear, measurable results.

VI. SOCIAL MEDIA

The creation of social media was truly a groundbreaking idea to connect people through a website platform. Think about all the money that has been spent from the late 90's though the early 2000's trying to get consumers' eyeballs on products. Nowadays, you can gain visibility for your products FOR FREE! And, better yet, social media allows for compounding visibility as your exposure increases exponentially whenever you add new friends, followers, or likes. All you need now is a little strategy and elbow grease to make the social networks work for you.

Yet, for the most part, frustration and disgust is the reaction we get from business owners about social media. Common questions we hear include: "What the heck is all this about social media and why should I care about it?" "Is any of this going to help my bottom line?" and "There are so many social media sites, which ones are important?" These are all good questions in the pursuit of a useful strategy regarding social media.

Social media is a marketing tool just like your website or your business cards. How you use it and what you put into the process of building your social network is where you will find an endgame. For example, social media is great for keeping your network updated on company news/awards and milestones. Our message is always to use each social media portal for what it is and don't try to make it what it is not.

Cultivating Your Brand[ed Traffic]

You hate social media because it is one more thing you aren't familiar with. Moreover, it is one more thing you need to worry about. You need it because in contemporary society, you must get and give information quickly. There is a market of customers on social media. They may not necessarily be in "buying mode" while they are snooping on other friends Facebook profiles or checking to see if Khloe Kardashian has tweeted in the last five minutes, but you can take advantage of their activity to create valuable positive impressions for your company.

Words, and the actions they describe, last forever on the internet. On the one hand, this may be frightening, but, on the other hand, if you embrace this fact you can benefit from it indefinitely. Knowing that your web presence is eternal should encourage you to be careful in protecting your reputation and conscientious in cultivating an image of yourself of which you can be proud. As an individual, your name is your brand. Have you ever Googled your own name? Try it now. Are you happy with what came up?

Whether you have or not is not a reflection of your vanity or lack thereof. People Google their own names all the time just to see what's out there about themselves. There's no need to fret if you were less than pleased with the search returns for your name – we can help you fix it.

Cultivating a name as a brand has been perfected by celebrities, and to them we now turn for some lessons:

The rise of social media has presented celebrities with an altogether new avenue of generating endorsement fees. Celebrities' respective social media pages have staggering amounts of followers, many of whom develop a level of trust in the celebrities by virtue of a perception that they have been granted an "inside peek" into the celebrities' lives. In the world of paid endorsements, the trust that celebrities cultivate through their various postings is the key to success. Celebrities (or the teams of people who work for them, more often than not) carefully manage the self-exploitation of their fame and reputation to ensure that they are only endorsing products or services that are consistent with the image they are trying to cultivate.[35] Moreover, celebrities (aside from, say, Samuel L. Jackson)[36] are careful to avoid diluting the value of their fame and reputation by over-endorsing products. By adhering to these threshold levels of discipline, celebrities maintain the value that their name can bring to certain products or businesses.

---

[35] For instance, you are unlikely to see a heartthrob male romantic comedy lead endorse the National Rifle Association. And, the people on whom he depends for his fame may not appreciate his love of Guns & Ammo Magazine, and so he protects his valuable image by not publicizing this part of himself.

[36] We love Sam, but have you seen the movies he's done lately? We're convinced he'll appear in any movie where the producers agree to meet his usual fee.

So what can we learn from this? First, we've learned that there is value in cultivating trust in your followers. Celebrities do this by sharing with their followers. For a business, the process is similar: provide your followers with good, meaningful content, and they will love you for it. People want a brand they trust to quench their thirst for knowledge. This harkens back to the desire to have a solid reputation. Consider giving away information free during a call-to-action. In exchange for emails or points of contact give away some of your expertise, so they will have a way of investing their trust in you. Information such as eBooks or downloadables allow a company to be a keynote speaker each time their words are read. A prime example is a book, which provides expert level information for the reader, and thus provides value to the reader. People love be "in the know" and they want to be up to date on the latest happenings. A company can increase its audience simply by appealing to these desires. The focus on content drives inbound marketing. Customers will engage with a business that provides them with valuable information. If you have good content, you can drive a customer to engage you with questions, or to seek your advice regarding a problem they may be having. Develop your content with this type of marketing strategy in mind.

Simple familiarity with a product or a business, and having a positive mental association with a product or business, is often enough to make a customer choose your product over another. People thrive on habit and will use a brand continuously if it has a positive association attached to it. Think of some of the products that have significant meaning for you. We always buy for a reason and purpose. The goal is to have rabid fans of your product. Word of mouth marketing is powerful and, if it is positive, your brand traffic will have a built in or loyal audience without too much effort.

People like to share good information about good products. Blogs, being platforms for people of varying influence to share their experiences, are powerful tools for marketers. There are blogs dedicated to just about every industry or product you can think of. Even things that you would think are unlikely to attract much attention can have blogs with huge followings. Even things like "a million and one uses for baking soda" or "the little black dress" have blogs with large followings.

If you look to large companies' use of marketing dollars to determine the desirability of different marketing practices, you will find that they invest heavily in the web. Clients ask us, especially during the sales process, "Why should I invest in the internet if my business does well without it?" Our response is always the same, "if you want to create a new source of revenues for your business, you should have a solid marketing plan angled towards expanding or creating your web presence."

When it comes to the long-term use of your marketing budget, there is no better place than search engines. One compelling reason for this is the permanent footprint of all work on websites/press releases and social media. Pages created on your site are indexed and stored on the servers of search engines forever. Not only will that digital file be there for people to find, but over time it gains trust with the search engines and, in turn, the search engine will promote it more highly. This is in stark contrast to print advertising. When you run an ad in a newspaper it is a one-shot deal. The paper gets distributed, and then likely finds its way to the trash, along with your lovely ad. Websites, like storefronts, are there as long as the business resides in that space. Just having a website without any custom digital marketing work can benefit your business. In a healthy campaign, half of all web traffic is brand traffic. Part of marketing is cultivating new clients while retaining old ones. The value of a lifelong customer is invaluable and speaks highly of the brand. Potential clients usually have a few impressions of you before considering a purchase. If they see positive reviews online and see your high ranking in search engines, they may convert without thinking about it. Brand traffic is crucial to building successful proprietary resources.

Don't Spend Too Much Time on Social Media

In the realm of time management, spending fifteen minutes thinking about a post for social media is not the best use of your time. Remember what social media is, insight into your life for others to see. Social media for business purposes is insight into your business for others to see. What always shocks us is that the analytics show that the most popular posts are always related to fleeting moments that are true representation of real life in your office. For example, a successful social media post can be little more than a person at their desk making a funny face or doing something goofy, or an individual winning an award or blowing out a birthday cake. These are the moments that make us relatable - moments all humans share.

A great use of time on social media is networking and growing your influence. We like to use Facebook as an example but almost all social media outlets have a tool to grow your network. That is how social media companies get bigger, by allowing their members to interact. Taking a few minutes to look to see if you can connect with people you know or want to know is a great practice for utilizing social media for your business, just don't spend hours on social media hoping that it is a cure-all.

Growth: Organic, Churning, and Purchasing

There are three methods of increasing your following on social media: organically, churning, and purchasing. Organically is by far the hardest. A new business will naturally have some growing pains on social media. Newcomers are treated with suspicion. People want to follow a trusted brand and a new brand is not to be trusted at first. Trust is earned one tweet at a time. The best way to organically earn Twitter followers is to find people in the same or related fields. A restaurant might want to follow other restaurants, silverware companies, or local farmers. Peers are generally as interested as you are in gaining followers and most will follow back. Peak hours for the site are between 10 am-4 pm. Promote your handle from business cards to business pages. Tweets should be of value and worthy of retweeting. Hashtags are signals/keywords to bring interested people to your profile. Finding your voice for Twitter is not always the easiest thing. If your goal is to entice people with an experience such as a trip or a six-course dinner, then do not come off as a schoolteacher. On the opposite end of the spectrum try to not use so much slang that only teenagers can decipher your tweets.

Consider how you want to come across and how people many perceive your voice. Your followers will grow with time. This brings up an interesting topic that no one wants to address head on. Should a startup purchase followers? For less than $5, you gain in numbers what might have taken you months to earn. Numerous celebrities have recently been called out for having fake followers, even President Obama has purchased most of his followers - over seventy percent of his forty million followers are fake or inactive accounts. While being called out for having fake followers is embarrassing, the top consideration should be your reputation. In countries where labor is cheap, people are hired to set up robotic accounts to generate followers. Some ask for your password when paying for the service. With them not only is your reputation at risk, but so is your credit card information. Low caliber people will use your account to spam your real followers, which never goes over well, and also to start phishing scams. Additionally, the people who create the fake accounts are generally not English speakers so the names they come up with can be ridiculous. Bucky McGee, Edible Swimsuit, or CDK5567 may follow you as a result. The internet has grown wise to these tricks and loves to call fakers out. It does come across as having to buy your friends.

Purchasing followers is not worth the risk to your reputation. Quality of followers is more important than the number of followers. Some bandwagon people may see you have impressive numbers and follow you, but it is unlikely that they will convert to customers - they just want to appear in the know. Twitter makes the temptation even sweeter by post numbers under the profile picture. Perhaps in the near future Twitter would make reference to people who are actually engaged with your product or service. Facebook, to be fair, has a way of seeing real participants by gauging the number of people who are talking about your page.

Churning is not as bad a practice as purchasing followers, but is still frowned upon. Twitter wants you to grow a following organically and does not want you to use shortcuts. Churning is simply following a large amount of people, waiting a few days while you hope they follow you back, and then unfollowing those that do not reciprocate. The wait can be as short as three days or as long as seven.

Spend no more than twenty minutes a day on social media. Gaining followers may feel as if you are moving your business forward, but if these are not interested followers than it doesn't matter the number count. The rule for social media is: quality over quantity.

Links from Social Media

Social media can also be a great source for links. Twitter started as a platform for celebrities, but now it connects business with potential clients and other businesses. There really is no secret to social media other than to get out there and connect. This isn't the high school lunchroom where everyone is divided and the cool kids will tell you that you can't sit with them. Most people are welcoming and as eager for followers as you are. Your presence should be a two-way conversation. Engage, but add value. Be easy to find and link everything back to your website. Make sure whatever you put out there is appropriate. If you are advertising to a specific group, make sure others will not be offended. Decide on a voice and use it consistently. The world is chaotic enough; your brand should be trustworthy and stable.

Make it easy to share content. Again, people always want to appear funny or smart. Install a share button so content can be shared and your site is seen as one of value. Research which social platforms your clients prefer. Certain demographics prefer certain social media channels.

Honesty

When considering what content to post on social media, the best plan is to take the honest Abe route. People love honesty! Take a look at the Newcastle Beer Campaign for example. One of their ads shows a freshly poured beer on a billboard with the caption: What makes Newcastle beer look so delicious? Its light brown color and Photoshop! This simple truth garners a reaction in people because of the outright honesty of the statement.

There is also humor in honesty. It's almost odd when someone is blatantly honest about something, and the unexpectedness of it can be very funny. The key is to pick something small and not serious. A bad example would be an honest post regarding your feelings about hot button political issues. A good idea would be the traffic on the way to work or how cold it was outside.

It's About People

The single most important thing to remember about social media is that it centers on people. If you remember nothing else from this book about social media, please remember that people are social animals and like to hear about other *people*. Always remember to that your social media posts should have a human element. For example:

- Joe's Autoworld is celebrating their 10th year in business (no human element)
- Joe and Mary from Joe's Autoworld would like to thank all their customers for a wonderful 10 years in business. Looking forward to the next 10! (human element)

By connecting a person to a business it becomes personal. Think about all the big companies you see advertising by adding a person to their company message. Many car dealerships place the owner out there just so you can see who is making money off your car. It is no longer a big corporate machine, but a person. Remember to make your postings about people and not your products or services.

VII. SEARCH ENGINES

"Does anyone know anything about Google?" We are sure this has been yelled across the office of many a business owner. Why? Usually it is because someone heard stories about their competition making money from the internet. Experienced, reputable companies are often confounded by the fact that relatively inexperienced competitors are out-marketing them. Google does not discriminate based on reputation or revenues. And, the search engine giant is continuously making its value known to new and different industries. If not by acquisitions, Google has organically grown into many industries. In the past, lawyers would not dare advertise with search engines. That was for ambulance chasing attorneys and traffic lawyers! Not anymore, large corporate law firms are investing millions into their websites and online platforms.

There is a simple explanation for this organic growth. It is something we have repeated many times to clients over the years. <u>You never know who is on the other end of the internet</u>.

How to Get in Their Good Graces

Stay away from any kind of tricks to cheat the system. Google has teams of people much smarter than you trying to figure out any shortcuts to search engine revenue. So, if tricks are out of the question, what is next? Here is the best part of doing business with the search engines: they give you the information you need to be successful. Google is one of the most forthcoming companies with proprietary information. Before you get excited, there is a difference between knowing what to do and knowing how to do it. What you can take from it is that by learning terminology and concepts of search marketing, you can set yourself apart as a business owner in the internet generation.

Another great way to get started is to understand who Google is and why they are such a big deal. Google is a gigantic internet library of information on every subject matter. The business model is simple. Google makes money by selling advertising on its search results. That is it! They use your information to make money. Knowing this is crucial to being successful because if you understand that by giving Google unique and relevant information about your business, they will reward you with more exposure online, you now understand the reciprocal relationship between Google and business owners.

The best practice to start a profitable relationship with Google is to research what makes them tick (relevant content) and to play by their rules without cutting corners. The flipside of this section is what happens when Google decides you have been cheating or are a fraudulent site. The term "Google-slapped" refers to when Google blocks a site from being displayed in its search returns because the site violated Google's guidelines in some way.

Many companies have been Google-slapped, particularly health and beauty products. One such salon had products on their site which were reevaluated by the FDA and prohibited for sale in the US. The company put a discontinued marker on their site. All was well, until one day it was not. Google will occasionally change its guidelines, and the markers were not up to snuff when this occurred. As a result, the company was Google-slapped. The company no longer appeared in Google's search returns – the kiss of death. Very little can be done once this happens. Read the entire policy even before you decide to advertise. Know what the limits and expectations are to save your business. Once you receive the violation notice, work with Google. They are helpful and do not want to lose business any more than you do. Go over your website, not just the ad in question. There are ways to manage it. Google will generally send out warnings to businesses. It is almost better to start over than try to fight Google. They always win.

Their Business is Your Business

It is easily forgotten that Google, Yahoo and Bing need you to survive. You are the business owner, the advertiser, and the consumer. They are looking to you to create the unique, rich, and relevant content to fill their search results. The entire purpose of search engines is to people find the information they are looking for. As a business owner, you are special in the eyes of the search engines because you are their source of revenues. The more money you make from Google, the more you will spend on Google advertising.

Breaking down the fear of the unknown with regards to search engines is step one for beginning to work with Google, Yahoo, and Bing. Search engines *need* the information you provide – give it to them in the right format and reap the rewards.

The Two Faces of Google Plex

We have to remind our clients all the time that Google is just looking to do business with you. Anyone who opens an advertising account (called an Adwords account) with Google can speak with a representative to learn about the best ways to format their advertising campaigns to increase their efficiency. However, while Google will give you advice, there is much about sound digital marketing practices that will be left out of the discussion.

What's the difference? The reps at Google are trained to encourage you to spend the most money possible on your account, while best practices digital marketing would aim to spend the least to get the most bang for your buck. How do you do that? Pay attention to what works. We always explain to prospective clients that Adwords should be set up using all the research tools available to you (Keyword Planner, Industry Jargon, Geo-Targeting, and even common sense). Once the campaign is live, taking advantage of what print and radio advertising do not have is key: look at your analytics. There are always trends in your campaigns that can be adjusted to produce the best results. Think of Adwords as a funnel. You begin with your best guesses and funnel what works through the analytics until you are left with a profit-producing campaign. Conceptually, this is the soul of Adwords' effectiveness.

Don't Forget Bing and Yahoo Just Because Everyone Else Has

Much of this book is about Google. Rightly so as they are the giant in the search marketing game. The numbers fluctuate, but Bing and Yahoo generally account for no more than thirty percent of all search marketing spend. What does this mean? By ignoring Bing and Yahoo, you are ignoring thirty percent of your target audience.

Let's talk for a second about well-rounded marketing campaigns. The digital world is about connection. The internet is computers connecting, while search engines are about websites connecting. Marketing on the internet should be about consumers connecting with your website from their computer (or mobile device). In the simplest possible form, the best way to market your business online is to make sure your business has exposure within every portal of the internet. What does this mean? Your website should be prevalent on Social Media, Email, and Search Engines. Branding is key, not just through search engines but through all forms of digital marketing. Your business should always look to any opportunities to have your brand noticed online. Converting strangers to customers is a tricky process.

The argument for including Yahoo and Bing into your digital strategy is not as much because of their large value as it is having a well-rounded approach to the internet. The other benefit is that Yahoo and Bing tend to be more affordable with respect to paid traffic than Google. They realize that they are far behind in the search marketing game and need to price themselves accordingly. To recap, advertise and optimize with Yahoo and Bing so you are capturing all 100% of your geo-search market, and because they are cheaper.

Pay Per Click

Organic listing can work, but when bills have to be paid, there is no better way than PPC. The goal with PPC is either lead generation or sales. This can be done one any type of budget. Big budgets ads will be shown more, thus have more impressions which can lead to more conversions. This enables bigger companies to have more of a buffer to test out ad groups or various types of advertising. Sales is primarily a numbers game, so the higher the number of impressions, the higher number of sales. Smaller budgets need to target wisely to save money.

PPC works for you as long as you work for it. You must have aware management, a strategy, and keyword optimization. Even if you hire a marketing team, you must be aware of your own advertising. They can do the work and strategize for you, but you ultimately are responsible for your success.

Keywords are essential. A popular keyword will have more clicks, and therefore cost more money. You must do your research beforehand on keywords that are relevant to your business. Google has a tool called Adwords Keyword Planner that is free for Gmail account holders. This will give you ideas for popular keywords. It will provide guidance for: broad match, broad match +modifier, phrase match, exact match, and negative match keywords. If you have a limited budget, seek out your core keywords. Vague keywords are a waste of money, and often a waste of a potential lead's time. Take your time with keywords and choose wisely.

Your paid ads have a set, four-line format: headline, descriptive line 1, descriptive line 2, and display url. This must be one cohesive unit and have synergy. Your descriptive lines set expectations and must be relevant. Don't be tempted to use your descriptive lines as a "bait and switch" to generate more traffic. It sets the stage for disappointment and is a complete waste of money.

A display url is your landing page. Set your goal with your landing page. Decide whether willit be to get emails through a call-to-action or to make a sale. Keep in mind that traffic coming from a search engine is unlikely to have any brand loyalty, and they would prefer for you to reach your point as quickly as possible.

Be aware in your strategy. The great thing about Google is you can select the hours your ad will be on display. This requires research and strategy. Are your clients early birds or night owls? Play around with times and see what works best. This is a great tool to take advantage of. You can even extend your ads to add information like your geographic location, which may increase your traffic. In addition, it gives your desired leads more reason to trust you. More information is not always better, but it can sometimes enhance your ad. You can add up to six extra pieces of information. This can include street address, with the option for directions, or the convenient call button that directly calls the number on your mobile. Keep in mind there is no added fee for ad extensions until your ad is clicked upon. To check if this is working for your business, Google keeps a tab for these extensions that you can monitor.

Ads with extensions tend to appear on the top of the pages rather than the sides to accommodate the added information, which can increase your click-through rate (CTR, remember?). If your ad does not make it to the top of the page, it will still be shown just not in a priority position.

VIII. Going Deeper Into the Data

Interpreting the data that is recorded from your site is not as black and white as people think. An increase in traffic sounds great, but what if there is not an increase in sales as well? What was the source of the traffic increase? What was the time of day? All of these questions will ultimately lead to better insight to your business online.

The key is to match your understanding of your business/industry with important patterns online. Nearly all business owners can tell you when their busy season is compared to a slow season. The same is true for internet marketers who are familiar in a specific industry. The ability to understand when/where to spend your money online is, many times, the difference between success and failure. There is no better asset to an internet marketer than the sharing of knowledge from the business owner. Their industry jargon, insight into seasons, and product knowledge is instrumental in creating a successful strategy.

Automation Saves Time and Your Business

When people hear automation, many times they think of their cable provider who is always trying to get them to sign up for their automated bill pay. There are good forms of automation, especially when it comes to website marketing. For instance, a business owner can set up automated reporting. Google Analytics will automatically generate reports for which you have provided guidelines. Online campaigns through search engines, display networks, or social media can be designed to turn off, turn on, or adjust appropriately. All without having to manually enter anything into the software. In addition, your website has automatic functionality depending on the platform used to create the site. Your website can send you an email every time a visitor has filled out a form or clicked on the phone number with a mobile phone.

These functionalities are all time saving software developments that can assist your marketing efforts. More importantly, the paid campaigns are a working progress. A good paid campaign professional will mold your campaign to spend the least to make the most. Once a campaign is running smoothly, those settings can be saved and the campaign will run automatically with set budgets and times of day to run. In the world of ecommerce, this is an automated revenue generator for your business. In lead generation, the phone will keep ringing with a solid campaign.

IX. Closing

Internet marketing is here to stay and adaption to it must happen right now. Google is a big help in any campaign, as is your marketing team. Invest money in big data, analytics, and insight into your business/target audience. Every dollar will be well spent in doing so. Spend the time getting to know the ins and outs of your chosen audience by doing research. Figure out what makes them tick and then weave your brand around them. Your brand belongs to them, not you, so entertain them. Be of value by making your content king. Answer their questions and address their pain points. They are coming to you seeking a solution, so be the authority that guides them to a comfort zone. Stay on top of your data and be current in all your research. If you hire a marketing team, treat them with the respect they deserve and accept that your business is ultimately your responsibility. Work hard, market wisely on the internet, and you will do steady business.

www.ingramcontent.com/pod-product-compliance
Lightning Source LLC
Chambersburg PA
CBHW051722170526
45167CB00002B/765